Servant of Yahweh

European University Studies
Europäische Hochschulschriften
Publications Universitaires Européennes

Series XXIII
Theology

Reihe XXIII Série XXIII
Theologie
Théologie

Vol./Bd. 848

PETER LANG
Frankfurt am Main · Berlin · Bern · Bruxelles · New York · Oxford · Wien

Antony Tharekadavil

Servant of Yahweh in Second Isaiah

Isaianic Servant Passages in Their Literary and Historical Context

PETER LANG
Internationaler Verlag der Wissenschaften

Bibliographic Information published by the Deutsche Nationalbibliothek
The Deutsche Nationalbibliothek lists this publication in the Deutsche Nationalbibliografie; detailed bibliographic data is available in the internet at <http://www.d-nb.de>.

ISSN 0721-3409
ISBN 978-3-631-57079-1

Printed in Germany 1 2 3 4 5 7

www.peterlang.de

Terminological Clarifications and Acknowledgements

There are certain frequently used words and concepts which call for explanation for the sake of clarity. By monotheism (monotheist) is here meant the worship of one deity as the only God and creator which implies the negation of the existence of all other deities. The word monolatry (monolatrous) means the worship of one God as the supreme and universal deity but it does not exclude the existence of other gods. Polytheism (polytheist) thinks of the existence of several gods and their power in the world. Both terms Israel and Judah unless specified or context clarifies refer to all the Babylonian exiles without difference of their origin because in the time of Second Isaiah the emphasis was on the exilic Jews rather than the division between the two Israelite kingdoms.

The English translations of the biblical texts in this book are done by the author himself after having consulted the translations like RSV and KJV.

I am grateful to God whose help and direction have been visible all through out my life. I express my sincere gratitude to my Archbishop His Grace Mar George Valiamattam. In express my sincere thanks to all my professors in Studium Biblicum Franciscanum in Jerusalem. I also thank my parents, my brothers, my sister, and all my friends and benefactors.

Table of Contents

Introduction

The Holy Week liturgy of several Christian Churches frequently reads and meditates on the so-called servant songs in Second Isaiah. Following the theological notions of the New Testament, the faithful Christians see the suffering and death of Jesus, the servant of God, as the fulfilment of the prophecies of the exilic prophet (cf. Act 3.13, 26; 4.27; compare with LXX Is 41.8; 42.1; 50.10; 52.13). Notably, John the Baptist pointed to Jesus as the "lamb of God who takes away the sin of the world" (Jn 1.29), which recalled the suffering servant of Yahweh who was mute like a lamb before its slaughterers (Is 53.7).

In fact, up to eighteenth century A.D., Christian writers, by and large, held the so-called fourth servant song (Is 52.13-53.12) as a messianic prophecy that found its fulfilment in Jesus Christ. Such a conception was also warranted because the whole Book of Isaiah (chapters 1-66) was then taken as the prophecy of the eighth century prophet (Isaiah of Jerusalem), which could on the one hand be relevant to the immediate hearers and on the other hand could find a fulfilment after centuries. There were several factors that prompted the early Christians to see Jesus of Nazareth as the fulfilment of the servant passages in Isaiah and as the expected Davidic messiah (Mic 5.2).

First, even though Jesus was able to do many amazing miracles including the raising of dead people, he had been totally quiet when he was betrayed and unjustly judged. The incredible silence of Jesus at the unjust judgement was one of the main reasons why the early church considered him as the servant of Yahweh (cf. 1Pet 2.22-25; compare with Is 53.4-7). This silence pointed to him as a credible teacher who was strong enough to hold on to his teaching of 'silent suffering before the persecutors': "I say to you, Do not resist one who is evil, but if any one strikes you on the right cheek, turn to him the other also" (Mt 5.39, 44).

Second, the kingdom of God was one of the important recurring themes in Jesus' teaching. He was always conscious of his duty of preaching the kingdom of God; for example according to the Gospel of Luke (4.43) he plainly declared: "I must preach the kingdom of God" (cf. also Mt 3.2; 4.17, 23; 5.3, 10; Mk 1.15; 4.11, 26; Lk 4.43; 6.20; Jn 3.3, 5; Act 1.3). As a result of his insistence on the need of preaching the kingdom, even his opponents - the Pharisees - were persuaded to ask him about the arrival of the kingdom (cf. Lk 17.20). In fact, the expectation that the 'elect' of Yahweh would be rescued and the everlasting kingdom of God would be established on earth was one of the expectations found in the pre-Christian Palestinian Pseudepigrapha (cf. for example Jubilees 1.28; 1Enoch 9.4; 12.3; 25.3-5, 7; 27.3; Test. of Moses 10.9; Test. of Dan 5.13; also Dan 2.44; 4.25).

Third, many of Jesus' words and actions had royal and messianic connotation: his Palm Sunday entry into Jerusalem had a royal appearance; his cleansing of the temple implied the authority of the expected messiah (Jn 2.13-22); his claim that he would rebuild the temple in three days raised eschatological hopes. The request of James and John that they should be granted the permission to sit at his right and left side also reflected this royal messianic conception (Mt 20.20-23). Jesus was truly a descendent of David born in the city of David (Mic 5.1; Mt 9.27). The messiah from the house of David, according to Jewish tradition, was expected to establish an eternal kingdom (Lk 1.32-33). In fact, Jesus was crucified as if he was a royal pretender (Mk 15.26; Jn 18.37; 19.21).

Fourth, Jesus often spoke of a father-son relationship that he had with God: "God so loved the world that he gave his only son that whoever believes in him should not perish but have everlasting life" (Jn 3.16; cf. also Mt 3.17; 4.3, 6; 11.27; 14.33; 16.16; 17.5; Mk 15.39; Lk 22.69-70; Heb 1.5; 5.5). To be labelled as the 'son of God' was in fact a royal privilege: the Davidic king was thought to be the son of Yahweh (2Sam 7.8-14; 1Chr 17.13; 22.10; 28.6; Ps 2.7; 89.27-28). The royal messiah should also be endowed with the spirit of Yahweh (Is 11.1-11); the servant of Yahweh of Isaiah was actually filled with the spirit (Is 42.1-4), so was also Jesus (Mt 3.16).

Even though Jesus' death apparently shattered the messianic promises (Mt 5.17-18; Lk 24.21), his resurrection helped the disciples to pick up where they left off (Rom 1.3-4). Jesus then commanded them to go to the ends of the earth and to announce his gospel (Act 1.8). These disciples had been the witnesses of the resurrection of their Lord (Mk 16.8, 14-18). They presented Jesus as the fulfilment of the divine promises: "we bring you the good news that what God promised to the fathers, this he has fulfilled to us their children by raising Jesus..." (Act 13.32-33).

The preaching of this gospel of resurrection however was not at all easy. The difficulty that the apostles faced from the non-Jews is clarified from the experience of Paul at Areopagus: "when they heard of the resurrection of the dead, some mocked; but others said, 'We will hear you again about this'" (Act 17.32). The problem to preach this message to the Jews was something different; for them the crucifixion of Jesus was a historical fact but about his resurrection there had been contradictory reports: the apostles reported that he was risen from the dead (Act 1.24, 32); the Jewish authorities and the soldiers who guarded the tomb, by contrast, reported that his body was stolen by his disciples (Mt 28.11-15).

In this confused situation, it was necessary for the early church to present Jesus as the long expected messiah and to say that his sufferings were only the fulfilment of the scripture (Act 2.23). They therefore sought scriptural texts with messianic expectations and interpreted the life of Jesus in the light of these texts. The servant passages in Second Isaiah were important texts in this regard.

Though Jesus is thus seen by the New Testament as the promised messiah and as the fulfilment of the Isaianic servant of Yahweh passages (cf. Act 8.27-39),[1] Second

[1] In fact, in the history of interpretation several persons and individuals have been identified as the suffering servant of Yahweh: the Book of Daniel (11.33-12.10), for example, interprets the Jewish loyalists in the period of persecution of the Antiochian period as the servant in Is 52.13-53.12 (cf. H. L. Ginsberg, "The Oldest Interpretation of the Suffering Servant," VT 3[1953], 400-404). The author of Enoch appears to have identified the servant with the Son of Man in the parables of Enoch: the Son of Man is the elect one (Enoch 40.5; 45.3; 46.3; 49.2; compare Is 42.1); he is

Isaiah himself regarded the Persian emperor Cyrus as the messiah and shepherd of Yahweh (44.28-45.1). This fact raises two questions: 1) what did the title 'messiah' mean in the time of Second Isaiah and in the exilic period and why did Second Isaiah call Cyrus the messiah of Yahweh? 2) If Cyrus was the messiah according to the prophet, who was the person behind the figure of the servant of Yahweh?

First, the idea of an anointed of Yahweh (משח) appeared with the emergence of the monarchy, and in the pre-exilic period the title "messiah" was primarily used to refer to the kings of Israel and Judah: it was often the synonym of the word king who was the anointed of Yahweh. See for example 2Sam 22.51: "Great triumphs he gives to *his king*, and shows steadfast love to *his anointed*, to David, and his descendants for ever" (see also 1Sam 2.10; Ps

---

the righteous one (Enoch 38.2; 46.3; compare Is 53.11); he is a light to the gentiles (Enoch 48.4; compare Is 42.6; 49.6); the Son of man will make the kings and the mighty stand up from their seats (Enoch 46.4; 53.3; compare Is 49.7; 52.15). The righteous man in the Wisdom of Solomon is a copy of Is 52.13-53.12 (Wis 3.1-6); The statement "I will allot him a portion with the many" in the Jerusalem Talmud (*Sheqalim* 5.1), according to the interpretation of Rabbi Jonah, refers to Rabbi Akiba who introduced the study of Midrash, Halakhoth, and Haggadoth. Several other Jewish authors thought that the servant was the 'wise': Jacob Ben Reuben, Eliezer of Beaujenci, and Aaron ben Joseph concluded from Dan 12.3 that the servant was the wise. Targum Jonathan ben Uzziel (1 A.D.?) identified the servant in Is 42.1; 43.10 and in 52.13-53.12 with the messiah; for a detailed discussion on the history of interpretation see C. R. North, *The Suffering Servant in Deutero-Isaiah.* A Historical Critical Study, 2nd ed. London, Oxford University, 1956, 7-11.

18.51); in another text, David said the following words to the inhabitants of Jabeshgilead, to those who buried the dead body of Saul: "Now, therefore, your hands will be strong, and be valiant; for Saul your lord is dead, and the house of Judah has anointed (משח) me king over them" (2Sam 2.4-7; see also 1King 1.34-35; 2King 11.12).

This anointed king was thought to be the vice-regent of Yahweh: "the kings of the earth will set themselves, and the rulers took counsel together, against Yahweh and his messiah..." (Ps 2.2). Yahweh's anointed person was also thought to be inviolable (1Sam 24.6, 10; 26.11; 2Sam 1.14-16; 19.21).[2] Up on his anointed, Yahweh bestowed his spirit (1Sam 11.6).[3] The duties of the royal messiah as underlined by Psalm 2 included just administration and deliverance of the people from their enemies. In fact, the first king Saul was anointed to be the ruler in Israel so that he should rescue them from the Philistines (1Sam 9.16; 10.1 cf. also 1Sam 11.8-9).

Exile was a comparable situation because the people of Yahweh were under distress due to the superiority of their enemies over them. The anointed king of Yahweh was no more. At this time, Second Isaiah saw the arrival of the victorious Cyrus who usually supported the local traditions and sanctuaries. The prophet was sure of the immi-

---

[2] See the discussion in M. De Jonge, "Messiah," *ABD* IV, 777-788; G. Stemberger, "Messias/Messianische Bewegung," *TRE* 22, 617-630; J. Tromp, "The Davidic Messiah in Jewish Eschatology of the First Century B.C.E," in *Restoration* (JSJSup 72), ed. J. M. Scott, Leiden, Brill, 2001, 191-194.

[3] Priests and prophets were also said to be anointed by Yahweh (cf. Lev 4.3, 5, 16; 6.22; 8.12; 1Chr 16.22; 1Chr 29.22; Ps 105.15; Dan 9.25-26).

nent liberation of the Judean exiles through this great emperor. Actually, he saw Cyrus as the redeemer sent by Yahweh because according to the prophet there was no other God who controlled the historical events (Is 44.24-28). As already mentioned, redemption of his people from their enemies was the first duty of the anointed of Yahweh. Notably, in Israel physical strength and military might were prerequisites for the recognition of a person as the anointed ruler/messiah of Yahweh (1Sam 10.23; 16.18; also Judg 6.12; 8.22).

The prophet therefore labeled this mighty foreigner as the messiah (redeemer) of Yahweh: "Thus said Yahweh to his anointed, to Cyrus" (45.1); "'he (Cyrus) shall build my city and set my exiles free, not for price or reward,' said Yahweh of hosts" (45.13); "For the sake of my servant Jacob, and Israel my chosen, I call you (Cyrus) by your name, I surname you, though you did not know me" (45.4). The prophet thought that Yahweh had given Cyrus universal authority. In addition, people really thought that Yahweh could anoint a person in order to fulfil certain tasks (1King 19.15-17; 2Chr 22.7).

Second, since the prophet called Cyrus the messiah and shepherd of Yahweh and he visualized a universal empire of Cyrus (41.1-4), it is clear that when the prophet organized his document (Is 40-53) and in it he gave an important emphasis to the figure of the servant of Yahweh, he was not thinking of the servant in the line of the Davidic messiah; he had someone else in mind. This prompts one to make an investigation into the person / persons behind the Isaianic servant figure that is often labeled as Israel but time and again appears to be someone different from Israel (cf. 49.3-5).

I

Historical Setting of the Servant Passages

The substantive *'ebed* (עֶבֶד, servant) occurs twenty times in Is 40-53 (in addition, the root *'bd* appears twice in a verbal form, 43.23, 24). Six times it occurs in the so-called four servant songs singled out by Bernhard Duhm (42.1-4; 49.1-6; *50.4-9*; 52.13-53.12). The originality of these four texts was first challenged by Duhm based on the notion that the figure of the servant of these poems differs significantly from the figure of the servant in the remaining parts of Second Isaiah (40-55).[4]

The suggestion of Duhm that separates these four songs from the Isaianic corpus and brings them under one heading called 'servant songs' is difficult to accept because according to the structure and form the so-called four servant songs are dissimilar. The first one is a monologue of Yahweh (42.1-4), in which he introduces his servant (behold, הֵן) to someone: here Yahweh labels his servant as his chosen one in whom he takes delight. The second one (49.1-6), a prophetic disputation, is a monologue of the servant: here the servant declares that Yahweh has formed him and then reproduces a dispute

---

[4] He also found stylistic differences between these four poems and the remaining Isaianic poetry; Duhm, *Das Buch Jesaia* (HKAT 3/1), Göttingen, Vandenhoeck & Ruprecht, 1968, 311.

between himself and Yahweh about his mission to the tribes of Israel and to the nations. The third song (50.4-9) is also a monologue of the servant which expresses his hope in Yahweh's redemption. The fourth song (52.13-53.12) consists of three comments: two of Yahweh and one of a group of people.

'What is common in these four so-called servant songs?' is not evident in such a way that one can separate them from the Isaianic corpus and bring them under a completely separate generic heading. The word *'ebed* does not even appear in all the texts: it does not appear in 50.4-9; the style of this poem is also different from other songs (see the repeated use of the syntagm Lord Yahweh [אֲדֹנָי יְהוִה] + verb + preposition [לִי] in vv 4-9). Neither the style, nor the speakers in them are the same. The themes are also different; moreover, according to some authors, there are more than four servant songs. For example, A. Laato speaks about eleven servant passages.[5]

Those scholars who followed Duhm and considered these four texts as a separate unit, tried to identify the figure behind these songs; subsequently, they pointed out to a number of individuals and groups as possible candidates.[6] Interestingly, in addition to the five collective

---

[5] *The Servant of YHWH and Cyrus* [CBOT 35], Stockolm, Almqvist & Wiksell, 1992, 69-156).

[6] For some of the recent interpretations of the servant songs cf. M. L. Barré, "Textual and Rhetorical-critical Observations on the Last Servant Song (Is 52:13-53:12)," *CBQ* 62 (2000), 1-27; C. Conroy, "The 'Four Servant Poems' in Second Isaiah in the Light of Recent Redaction-Historical Studies," in *Biblical and Near Eastern Essays*, FS J. Cathcart, ed. C. C. McCarthy and J. F. Healey (JSOT-Sup 375), Edinburgh, T&T Clark, 2004, 80-94; E. Cortese, *La*

interpretations (i.e., the servant is the Collective Israel, he is the Ideal Israel, the Remnant of Israel, the Prophets in Israel, and the Priests), sixteen individual names of historical figures have been suggested as possible candidates: Hezekiah, Isaiah, Uzziah, Josiah, Jeremiah, Moses, Sheshbazzar, Zerubbabel, Nehemiah, Jehoiachin, Eleazar, Ezekiel, Cyrus, Job, Meshullam, and Zedekiah.[7]

---

preghiera del re: Formazione, redazione e teologia dei 'Salmi di Davide' (SRB 43), Bologna, EDB, 2004, 54-57; "Il 'Servo di JHWH' (SdJ)," *RStB* 14 (2002), 81-98; B. C. De Vaux Saint-Cyr, C. Defelix, and J.-N. Guinot, *El Siervo Doliente (Isaias 53)* (DTB 32), Estella, Verbo Divino, 2004; E. R. Ekblad, Jr., *Isaiah's Servant Poems According to the Septuagint* (CBET 23), Leuven, Peeters, 1999; M. D. Goulder, "Behold My Servant Jehoiachin," *VT* 52 (2002), 175-190; G. P. Hugenberger, "The Servant of the Lord in the 'Servant Songs' of Isaiah: A Second Moses Figure," in *The Lord's Anointed*, ed. P. E. Satterthwaite, et al., Carlisle, Paternoster, 1995, 105-140; G. A. F. Knight, *Servant Theology.* A Commentary on the Book of Isaiah 40-55 (ITC 29/2), Grand Rapids, Eerdmans, 1984; Niccacci, "Quarto carme del Servo del Signore (Is 52,13-53,12): Composizione, dinamiche e prospettive," *LA* 55 (2005), 9-26; P. W. D. Paton-Williams, "The Servant Songs in Deutero-Isaiah," *JSOT* 42 (1988), 79-102; G. J. Polan, "Portraits of Second Isaiah's Servant," *BT* 39 (2001), 88-93; J. Werlitz, "Vom Gottesknecht der Lieder zum Gottesknecht des Buches," *BK* 61 (2006), 208-211.

[7] For the past attempts to identify the servant see the already mentioned detailed study of North, *The Suffering Servant.* Cortese ("Il Servo," 81-98.) and some others see the humiliated Zedekiah or the Judean King in the servant figure. There is another Messianic interpretation (P. Grelot, "Serviteur de JHWH," *DBS* XII, 958-1016) and the unknown teacher of the Law of Duhm (*Das Buch*, 379). Many of these individual interpretations are not accepted by recent scholars.

This abundance of hazy proposals about the identity of the servant of Yahweh of these four Isaianic poems shows that the act of taking away these poems from their present literary contexts has not resolved any of the problems related to the interpretation of these poems; moreover, as already mentioned, the noun *'ebed* (עֶבֶד), that appears only in the singular in Second Isaiah,[8] does not appear in the so-called third servant song (50.4-9). In the occurrences of the noun (*'ebed*) outside these servant songs, in fact, the single noun explicitly refers to Israel as the servant of Yahweh (except one text, 49.7); the second servant song also agrees with this point because it also calls Israel as the servant of Yahweh ("He said to me, 'You are my servant, Israel, in whom I will be glorified,'" 49.3).[9]

Since the suggestion to give special status to the so-called four servant songs is neither based on vocabulary nor based on style, and since the noun *'ebed* is identified as Israel in several Isaianic passages including the so-called servant songs, we read the four servant songs (Duhm) as integral parts of Second Isaiah. A rhetorical reading also suggests such a consideration. As a result, we count twelve passages in which the term servant

---

[8] The present author delimits the text of the exilic prophet to Isaiah chapters 40-53; cf. A. Tharekadavil, "Monotheism, Redemption, and the Formation of Israel as the Servant of Yahweh," Thesis ad Doctoratum, Jerusalem, SBF 2007, 13-19.

[9] The elimination of יִשְׂרָאֵל (v 3) as gloss is not supported by any of the ancient texts; cf. also N. Lohfink, "'Israel' in Jes 49,3," in *Wort, Lied und Gottesspruch.* Beiträge zu Psalmen und Propheten (FB 2), ed. J. Schreiner and J. Ziegler, Würzburg, Echter Verlag, 1972, 217-229.

(*'ebed*) appears (except 51.1-3) as Isaianic servant texts (41.8-9; 42.1-4, 18-25; 43.10-13; 44.1-5, 21-22, 24-28; 49.1-6; 48.20-21; 50.4-11; 51.1-3; 52.13-53.12) and tries to interpret these passages in relation to other Isaianic texts in their historical and conceptual context.

Notably, some of the Isaianic texts clearly address the exilic Israel as the chosen Servant of Yahweh: "But you, Israel, are my servant, Jacob, whom I have chosen, the offspring of Abraham, my friend; you whom I have strengthened from the ends of the earth, and called from its farthest corners, saying to you, 'You are my servant, I have chosen you and did not cast you off'" (41.8-9; also 49.3-6). The idea of election and strengthening from *the ends of the earth* shows that the servant motif should be interpreted in the Babylonian exilic context. The Babylonian context is also clarified by other texts; for example, Is 48.20 explicitly calls the servant to go out of Babylon: "Go forth from Babylon, flee from Chaldea, declare this with a shout of joy, proclaim it, send it forth to the end of the earth; say, 'Yahweh has redeemed his servant Jacob.'"

In some other texts, the servant motif is linked with pro-Yahweh monotheism: "'You are my witnesses,' said Yahweh, 'and my servant whom I have chosen, that you may know and believe me and understand that I am He; before me no god was formed, nor shall there be any after me ..." (43.10-13; cf. also 45.4-7). The Isaianic servant motif should therefore be discussed in the context of the monotheistic theology of Second Isaiah.

As a matter of fact, even when several Isaianic texts explicitly present the exilic Israel as the obedient and suffering servant of Yahweh (e.g., 49.3), some other texts present this Israel as blind, deaf, and unwilling to obey Yahweh's commandments (e.g., 42.18-25). There exists thus a difference between the servant Israel and the rest of Israel (See for example Is 49.5: "Now thus said Yahweh who formed me from the womb to be his servant, to bring Jacob back to him, and that Israel might be gathered to him ..."). This in fact led several scholars, as mentioned above, to look for a specific individual in the servant figure, who is different from Israel. The past attempts in this line, however, did not show any scholarly consensus. This point demands a detailed analysis of the Isaianic concept of the servant of Yahweh in the historical setting of the Isaianic text. Actually, the servant often represents the exilic Israel but sometimes appear to represent a particular person or persons different from the rest of Israel.

Procedure

In Second Isaiah Yahweh calls the exiles his servant and assures them victory over their enemies (cf. 41.8-16). Actually, religious notions of the ancient world were basically linked with political and social concepts. Since the Isaianic message was spoken to the exilic Israel who had lost their political, religious, and social set up, we will first look into the political situation in the last years before the fall of Jerusalem and the political conceptions of the ancient Near East shared by the pre-exilic and exilic Israel; when their political and cultic system collapsed, the theologians had to reinterpret the traditional religious notions. We will therefore look into the relevant traditional notions of Israel that the exilic theologians had to reinterpret in order to revive the religion. We will also see the religious conceptions of the Babylonians that affected this reinterpretation.

First we will briefly discuss the political and conceptual setting of the exilic Israel as reflected in the Isaianic text and then will analyze all the relevant Isaianic passages that seem to help the understanding of the Isaianic 'servant of Yahweh' concept in its historical-political, religious, and cultural context.

A. Political Situation

In the late seventh century and in the first half of the sixth century B.C., four rival political powers existed in the ancient Near East: Lydia (Mermnad dynasty of West Asia Minor, 685-547 B.C.), Media (Iranian kingdom), Babylon, and Egypt.[10] Babylon became most powerful under Nebuchadnezzar (604-562 B.C.) who rebuilt the empire (Neo-Babylonian Empire).[11] After having signed a treaty of peace with Media, Babylon turned its attention to Palestine and Egypt. Now, Egypt consolidated its power in order to meet the looming threat. The neighboring small kingdoms had to make alliances with one of these powers in order to evade destruction and deportation of its population.

Actually, the military power of the great emperors decided the existence, stability, and growth of the smaller kingdoms. Notably, according to the ancient Near Eastern conception, every kingdom on earth belonged to its national god who dwelt in the heavens; wars, victories, and failures of the kingdoms on earth were only reflections of what was going on in the heavens -- what was going on

---

[10] B. K. McLauchlin, "Lydia," *ABD* IV, 423-25; T. C. Young, Jr., "Media," *ABD* IV, 658-59.

[11] B. T. Arnold, "What has Nebuchadnezzar to do with David? On the Neo-Babylonian Period and Early Israel," in *Mesopotamia and the Bible* (JSOTSup 341), ed. M. W. Chavalas and K. L. Younger Jr., Sheffield, SAP, 2002, 339-344.

between the gods (cf. Deut 32.8-9).[12] In fact, the little Palestinian kingdom Judah had been vacillating between Babylon and Egypt with an eye on the timely advantages resulted from the competition between these superpowers (Jer 2.18, 36; Hos 7.11).[13]

At this time, there were two political groups in Judah: one that preferred the alliance with Babylon (like prophet Jeremiah), and the other that favored allegiance with Egypt (like prophet Hananiah; cf. Jer 27-28; 37.11-16).[14] Even though Egypt reinforced its military might under Pharaoh Neco (609-595 B.C.) and controlled Palestine

---

[12] Cf. P. R. Ackroyd, "The Temple Vessels: A Continuity Theme," in *Studies in the Religious Tradition of the Old Testament* (VTSup 23), London, Brill, 1972, 166-181; B. Becking, "Assyrian Evidence for Iconic Polytheism in Ancient Israel?," in *The Image and the Book* (CBET 21), ed. K. van der Toorn, Leuven, Uitgeverij Peeters, 1997, 161; M. D. Coogan, "Canaanite Origins and Lineage: Reflections on the Religion of Ancient Israel," in *Ancient Israelite Religion*, ed. F. M. Cross et al., Philadelphia, Fortress, 1987, 115-124; H. Frankfort, *Kingship and the Gods*, Chicago, University of Chicago, 1971, 241; P. Gerlitz, "Krieg: Religiongeschichtlich," *TRE* XX, 12; T. Vuk, "Wiedererkaufte Freiheit: Der Feldzug Sanheribs gegen Juda nach dem Invasionsbericht 2 Kön 18, 13-16", Thesis ad Lauream, Pars dissertationis, SBF, 1984, 50-53, 61-63, 65; "Religione Nazione e Stato," *LA* 40 (1990), 125-128.

[13] A. Malamat, *History of Biblical Israel* (CHANE 7), Leiden, Brill, 2001, 325-337.

[14] The existence of small and conflicting kingdoms in the region was probably a benefit for Egypt: through such small kings, it could retain its dominion in the region, and get tribute without any risk.

(2King 23.31-35; 2Chr 36.1-4),[15] it was defeated by Nebuchadnezzar in the war of Charchemish in 605 B.C. (Jer 46.1-12), and was subsequently kept away from Palestine; thus, Judah became a vassal of Babylon and remained faithful to that power until the next Egyptian incursion (Jer 25.1-11; 36.1).[16]

In 601-600 B.C., Pharaoh Neco II invaded Judah and captured Gaza.[17] The Judean King Jehoiakim, then, joined with Egypt neglecting the pro-Babylonian counsel of Jeremiah (cf. Jer 25.1-25). In 598 B.C., Nebuchadnezzar began a military expedition to suppress all the rebels in the region; he came to Jerusalem, and besieged it.[18] Unexpectedly, the Judean king died during this siege or after the city had been conquered;[19] his son Jehoiachin

---

[15] T. R. Hobbs, "Neco," *ABD* IV, 1060-61; A. Gardiner, *Egypt of the Pharaohs*, London, Clarendon, 1961, 267-79.

[16] In 601 B.C. Babylon invaded Egypt but lost before the forces of Pharaoh; this event gave Egypt another chance to control Palestine; cf. O. Lipschits, *The Fall and Rise of Jerusalem. Judah Under Babylonian Rule*, Winona Lake, Eisenbrauns, 2005, 364.

[17] D. L. Smith-Christopher, "Reassessing the Historical and Sociological Impact of the Babylonian Exile (597/587-539 BCE)," in *Exile: Old Testament, Jewish, and Christian Conceptions* (JSJSup 56), ed. J. M. Scott, Leiden, Brill, 1997, 13; J. A. Soggin, *Storia d'Israele* (BCR 44), Brescia, Paideia, 1984, 374.

[18] J. Finegan, *Handbook of Biblical Chronology,* Princeton, University Press, 1964, 198-209; L. Mazzinghi, *Storia di Israele* (MB 4), Casale Monferrato, Piemme, 1992, 98-99; D. J. Wiseman, *Chronicles of Chaldaean kings (626-556 B.C.) in the British Museum*, London, Trustees of the British Museum, 1956.

[19] With regard to the death of Jehoiakim, there are conflicting reports: according to 2King 24.6 he probably had a natural death ("he slept with his ancestors"); the Lucianic recension of 2King

(Coniah) took power as the new king (2King 24.6-17; Jer 22.24-30; 2Chr 36.9-10).

Nebuchadnezzar deposed the new king and exiled him as a prisoner to Babylon; however, in Babylon this king was respectfully treated (2King 25.27-30; Dan 1.1-2). Nebuchadnezzar also carried off all the treasures in the temple of Yahweh and in the Judean palace (2King 24.13); moreover, all the officials, artisans, smiths, warriors, and all men of valor were exiled to Babylon (2King 24.15-16); prophet Ezekiel was one among these deported (2King 24.14; Ezek 1.1-2).[20] Nebuchadnezzar made Mattaniah, the uncle of Jehoiachin, the king of Judah and changed his name to Zedekiah (2King 24.17). He was an unstable and inefficient king (cf. Jer 37-38).

In 594-593 B.C., Zedekiah sponsored an anti-Babylonian alliance of the local kings and rebelled against Babylon under the compulsion from Egyptian Pharaoh Psammetichus II (595-589 B.C.) who sought control over the region (Ezek 17.15).[21] To Zedekiah's misfortune, this

---

24.6 adds that he was buried in the garden of Uzzah; 2Chr 36.6, by contrast, reports that Nebuchadnezzar bound him in fetters to take him to Babylon; according to Josephus (*Ant*, 10.6), the king was killed in Jerusalem at the command of Nebuchadnezzar.

[20] The number of the deportees according to 2King 24.14 was ten thousand; according to 24.16, it was eight thousand, and according to Jer 52.28, it was about three thousand and twenty three; thus, the exact number was unknown. Cf. Smith-Christopher, "Reassessing," 14-15; M. Cogan, *Imperialism and Religion* (SBLMS 19), Missoula, Scholars Press, 1974, 99-103.

[21] Probably at this time the Egyptian party became stronger in Judah (cf. Jer 27-28); G. W. Ahlström, *The History of Ancient Palestine From the Palaeolithic Period to Alexander's Conquest* (JSOTSup 146), Sheffield, JSOT, 1993, 793-795.

coalition did not succeed; subsequently, he sent a delegation to Babylon and remained subject to that emperor (Jer 29.3). Later, however, in 589-588 B.C., he rebelled once again against Babylon by making alliance with Egypt (then ruled by Pharaoh Hophra, 589-570 B.C.) and other local kings.

By then, the division between the two political factions within Judah became more prevailing: the pro-Egyptian group was sustained by the army and some of the prophets, and it held the theology of the inviolability of the temple of Yahweh and the inevitable return of the exiles (cf. Jer 5.12; 14.13; 7.26, 28); the other group, which included Jeremiah, still preferred the allegiance to Babylon as functional (Jer 26.20-24; 37.5-7; 43.8-13; 44.30; 46.13-25; Ezek 29.17-20; 30.10-12, 24-25). At this time, with the hope of strengthening the army, Judah also liberated all the Jewish slaves (Jer 34.8-22).

In 587 B.C., probably in January, Nebuchadnezzar came to suppress the rebellion and besieged Jerusalem (2King 25.1-7; Jer 39.1-14; 52.1-28; 2Chr 36.14-21).[22] This siege lasted for about one and a half year. Pharaoh Hophra then sent a force to help the Judeans; subsequently, Babylonians lifted their siege for a short time in order to nullify Pharaoh's plans (Jer 37.5-10). Judeans, then, arrested the pro-Babylonian Jeremiah accusing him of deception and providing intelligence to the enemies (Jer 25.9; 27.6; 43.10; 37.11-15).

---

[22] About a number of opinions and discussion on the exact date of the coming of Nebuchadnezzar cf. Lipschits, *The Fall*, 366; Soggin, *Storia d'Israele*, 376-77; see for bibliography and comments Ackroyd, *Exile and Restoration*, 20.

Unfortunately, even with all his shrewdness, Zedekiah could not escape from Nebuchadnezzar's might; the besieged city went into starvation (2King 25.3). The Babylonian emperor captured Zedekiah in the plains of Jericho as he tried to flee from the Holy City into Arabah, probably to escape to Ammon (Jer 39.2; 52.6-11; 2King 25.3-5); the soldiers of Zedekiah fled (Jer 52.8); Nebuchadnezzar then slaughtered the sons of Zedekiah before his own eyes, then he put out his eyes and exiled him to Babylon (2King 25.6-7; Jer 39.5-7). In July 586 B.C., after having taken the valuable things inside the temple in Jerusalem, Babylonians burned it; they also destroyed the walls of the city (2King 25.8-10, 13-17, 18-23; Jer 39.8; 52.14).[23]

As disaster followed one after the other, in the eyes of the people, in fact, it was not Yahweh whose decisions directed the events; it was rather the dominating emperor who decided the matters in the world which included even the destruction of the temple of Yahweh.[24] Second

---

[23] The Edomites in the south then took advantage of the situation and plundered the cities of Judah (cf. Ps 137.7; Lam 4.21-22; Ezek 25.12-14).

[24] For example, Ahaz was subject to Assyria, and thus saved the kingdom from destruction (cf. 2King 16.3); Hezekiah who organized rebellion had lost 46 walled cities and had to pay a heavy tribute to Assyria (2King 18.13-16); Josiah -- hailed as a reformer -- had died in the Battle against the Egyptians making a historical change in the history of Judah's international relations (2King 23.28-34); Manasse, though accused of idolatry by the Biblical authors, ruled Judah for 55 years because he remained subject to Assyria (2King 21.3); even though the territory was limited, under him Judah thrived more than before; cf. Cogan, *Imperialism*, 66-75, 95; Lipschits, *The Fall*, 360-361.

Isaiah's depiction of Yahweh as the mighty emperor and warrior (e.g., 40.23; 42.13) and Israel as his servant accompanied with a military language of violence should be understood in this political and conceptual milieu: "But you, Israel, ... You are my servant ... fear not, for I am with you ... I will strengthen you ... I will uphold you with my victorious right hand ... those who strive against you shall be as nothing and shall perish... Behold, I will make of you a threshing sledge, new, sharp, and having teeth; you shall thresh the mountains and crush them, and you shall make the hills like chaff..." (41.8-16).

Babylon thus conquered Judah once again. With this conquest, one more group of officials and artisans were deported to Babylon (2King 25.11).[25] Jeremiah still remained in the land because being a pro-Babylonian he had the choice either to do so or to go with the Babylonians (Jer 40.1-6). Nebuchadnezzar, then, appointed Gedaliah, a local noble (probably a pro-Babylonian), as the ruler of Judah. The new ruler administered the land from Mizpah (Tel en-Nasbeh - six miles north-west of Jerusalem; that means Zion - the seat of Yahweh - was destroyed) and had to be unconditionally faithful to the Emperor (Jer 40.5-7; 2King 25.22-26).

The Babylonians also distributed the land to the remaining poor local (2King 25.12; Jer 39.10; 40.10; Ezek 11.15; 33.24) and foreign population (Lam 5.2) who were under the authority of this new governor (Jer 39.10;

---

[25] The version of the Chronicler that 'those remnant which had escaped from the sword were taken to Babylon' cannot be interpreted literally (2Chr 36.20).

52.16; see also Ezek 33.21-27).[26] This system, however, did not last long: due to reasons unknown, an Ishmael of the royal family killed the new governor (2King 25.25-26; Jer 40.1-41.10) after which another part of the population left the land for Egypt seeking a more secure life.[27] Others still remained in the ruined land in Judah and Samaria (Ezek 33.24; Jer 41.5), and there were probably still certain cultic services going on in the place of the Judean temple.[28]

With these exiles, even though the number was not so high, practically all the elite people in the Judean community, 'the Judaism of the time,' was transferred to Babylon (the officials, priests, and all the educated). These exiles settled in the areas by the Chebar River (Tel Abib, Tel Melah, Tel Harsha, Cherub, Addan, and Immer; Ezek 1.2-3; 3.15; Ezra 2.59; Neh 7.61).

---

[26] When the exiles returned, they demanded the restitution of their land which created further problems (cf. Neh 5.1-13; cf. Ezek 11.15; 33.24).

[27] This portion of the people, against the council of Jeremiah (Jer 42-43), migrated to Egypt and settled in Migdol, Tahpanhes (Daphne), and Memphis (Jer 44.1; 46.14; Jer 2.16; 46.14, 19; Ezek 30.13; Hos 9.6 [Memphis]; Ezek 29.10; Ex 14.2; Num 33.7 [Migdol]; Jer 43.8-13 [Tahpanhes]).

[28] According to Jer 41.5, after the fall of Jerusalem, eighty mourning men went to Jerusalem in order to offer gifts - offerings - to Yahweh in the destroyed temple. The Babylonian intention was only to destroy Judah as a military base; however, the temple was burnt, the bronze pillars and the ark were destroyed (2King 25.9, 13-15); cf. Ackroyd, *Exile and Restoration*, 25, 29-30; Lipschits, *The Fall*, 369; Soggin, *Storia d'Israele,* 384-85. The ark had probably been removed by Manasseh; cf. M. Haran, "The Disappearance of the Ark," *IEJ* 13 (1963), 46-58.

The nobility and high class of the population subsequently lived around 50 years there. Even in exile, they considered themselves as the better part of Israel (the elect, Jer 24.1-9; compare Ezekiel 11.14-21; Ezra 9.1-4). Second Isaiah repeatedly calls the exilic Jacob-Israel the chosen one of Yahweh (41.8, 9; 43.10; 44.1, 2; 48.10; 49.7; cf. 42.1; 43.10; 45.4).

Unlike the Assyrians, Babylonians did not disperse the exiles, but allowed them to live as small communities and permitted them to have a certain amount of religious organization like the office of the elders (Jer 29.1; Ezek 8.1; 14.1; 20.1). The life in Babylon under the protection of the great emperor gave them more security than their life in the little and dependent Judah, where social safety was always at risk. They could build houses, buy land, live as families (Jer 29.4-9), and had contact with their homeland (Jer 29.1). All these opportunities seem to have led them to economic prosperity in a short time. The liberation of the Judean King Jehoiachin from prison by the Babylonian emperor points to the freedom enjoyed by the exiles (2King 25.27-30).

The life as a community with at least some of their traditional offices (Jer 29.1; Ezek 3.15; 8.1; 14.1; 33.30-33) also gave them the chance to worship their own God as a community: actually they were not forced to worship the Babylonian gods. The economic prosperity and the possibility to have community life and worship also seem to have prompted many Jews later to remain in Babylon instead of returning to the homeland;[29] moreover, their properties in Judah were already occupied by others.[30]

Even when the exiles were economically sound, the exile was a wound to the nation. They had lost not only their homeland and often dearest family members, but also their status as important members of the society; they also lost their temple (Ps 137). The exilic prophets (Jeremiah, Ezekiel, Second Isaiah) and Deuteronomistic theologians then interpreted exile as the punishment of Yahweh for the idolatry of Israel (1King 9.7-9; 2King 17.14-18; 21.10-15) and announced the restoration of their temple, the cult, and the nation (Ezek 40-48; Is 44.28; 45.13). The national wound suffered by the intellectual section of this society, together with economic prosperity, security, and freedom helped them -- spiritually and materially -- to revitalize their religion.[31] They were also responsible to collect and edit many of the biblical traditions.[32]

---

[29] Josephus, *Ant,* 11. 8; Soggin, *Storia d'Israele*, 396.

[30] After the Babylonian conquest and deportation, the land had been distributed to the poor local population (Jer 39.10 [52.16]; 2King 25.12); the remaining land might have also been occupied by others.

[31] Cf. R. Albertz, *A History of Israelite Religion in the Old Testament Period.* From the exile to the Maccabees, trans by J. Bowden (OTL), Louisville, John Knox, 1994, 373-377.

[32] Cf. 1King 8.46-51; 9.7ed-9; 2King 17.14-18; 21.10-15; S. L. McKenzie, "Deuteronomic History," *ABD* II, 165; G.E. Mendenhall, *Ancient Israel's Faith and History.* An Introduction to the Bible in Context, Louisville, John Knox, 2001, 183-184; Soggin, *Storia d'Israele*, 380; H. Vorländer, "Der Monotheismus Israels als Antwort auf die Krise des Exils," in *Der Einzige Gott*, ed. Lang, B.,

In the absence of the temple and cult the practice of circumcision, observance of the Sabbath, and customs and rules in relation to food received exceptional value because they in a certain way demonstrated the Jewish national and ethnic identity.[33] Probably, this was also the time of the origin of the synagogues (not as special buildings)[34] because people needed a place to come together for prayers and scripture reading:[35] without such

---

et al., München, Kösel Verlag, 1981, 97; J. A. Sanders, "The Exile and Canon Formation," in *Exile* (JSJSup 56), ed. J. M. Scott, Leiden, Brill, 1997, 37-62.

[33] Soggin, *Storia d'Israele*, 381-82; M. Clauss, *Geschichte Israels.* Von der Frühzeit bis zur Zerstörung Jerusalems (587 v. Chr.), München, Beck, 1986, 205. In fact, the Book of Ezekiel gives most of the biblical references to Sabbath (20.12-24; 22.8-26; 23.38; 44.24; 45.17; 46.1-4, 12; cf. 2Chr 36.21).

[34] F. Castel, *Storia d'Israele e di Giuda, dalle origini al II secolo d. C.*, 2nd revised ed. (GB 5), Torino, Paoline, 1987, 126; Albertz, *A History*, 508; E. M. Meyers, "Synagogue," *ABD* VI, 252. In fact, as Meyers says, it is difficult to produce documentary evidence for the origin of synagogues; for discussion and different suggestions on the origin and development of synagogues see L. J. Hoppe, *The Synagogues and Churches of Ancient Palestine*, Collegeville, Liturgical Press, 1994, 7-14; L. I. Levine, *The Ancient Synagogue*, New Haven, Yale University, 1999; B. Olsson and M. Zetterholm, ed. *The Ancient Synagogue from its Origins until 200 C.E.* (CBNT 39), Stockholm, Almquist & Wiksell, 2003; A. Runesson, *The Origins of the Synagogue* (CBNT 37), Stockholm, Almquist & Wiksell, 2001.

[35] Like the Jewish settlers in Elephantine, most probably, the Jews in Babylon had built a cultic centre. During the time Ezra, actually, there existed a cultic centre (Casiphia) which might have been only the continuation of the old institution: here Ezra could recruit cult personnel (Ezra 8.15-20): "(Ezra) sent them to Iddo, the leading

religious gatherings, the act of maintaining the traditional faith would have been impossible for such a long time.

The Jews at this time adopted the Babylonian calendar. Still the most important thing was the influence of Aramaic. This language was then in the process of becoming an international means of communication. Israelites in exile adopted the Aramaic alphabet (instead of Phoenician); Aramaic also substituted Hebrew in the everyday life; even then Hebrew was preserved in the cult and in theological discussions. In fact, the scribes in the post-exilic period had to invent a new language (i.e., the late Biblical Hebrew) in order to maintain the traditional vernacular at least in the literary realm.

The destruction of the monarchy, the temple, and the exile of the population from the Promised Land seriously affected the traditional faith and conceptions about the promises of their national deity, Yahweh. According to their tradition, Yahweh had called Abraham and promised the land as a possession to his descendants: "On that day Yahweh made a covenant with Abram, saying, 'To your descendants I give this land, from the river of Egypt to the great river, the river Euphrates,'" (Gen 15.18).

Similarly, according to the traditional faith, Moses, the servant of Yahweh, had liberated Israel from Egypt, and Yahweh through Moses had promised them the land of

---

man in Casiphia, the place (הַמָּקוֹם), telling them what to say to Iddo and his brethren the temple servants at the place Casiphia, namely, to send us ministers for the house of our God" (V 17); see the discussion on the possible existence of a sanctuary in L. E. Browne, "A Jewish Sanctuary in Babylonia," *JTS* 17 (1916), 400-401; A. Cowley, "The Meaning of מָקוֹם in Hebrew," *JTS* 17 (1916), 174-176.

Canaan as a perpetual possession: "I will bring you into the land which I swore to give to Abraham, to Isaac, and to Jacob; I will give it to you for a possession. I am Yahweh." (Ex 6.8). In addition, Yahweh told Moses in the plains of Moab: "Say to the people of Israel, When you pass over the Jordan into the land of Canaan, then you shall drive out all the inhabitants of the land from before you, ... and you shall take possession of the land and settle in it, for I have given the land to you to possess it" (Num 33.51-53).

Since the tradition of the promise of the land is discussed by several biblical traditions, we can say that it was an integral part of their faith. For example, Deuteronomist reports the following words of Moses: "Behold, I have set the land before you; go in and take possession of the land which Yahweh swore to your fathers, to Abraham, to Isaac, and to Jacob, to give to them and to their descendants after them" (Deut 1.8); The Psalmist sings the same tradition in these words: "He drove out nations before them; he apportioned them for a possession and settled the tribes of Israel in their tents." (Ps 78.55). Following the direction of Moses and Joshua, Israel took possession of this land (Deut 34.5; Josh 5.14; 24.29).

Later, in the course of history, Israel grew into a monarchy; then the Davidic king received another important divine promise which assured him an eternal throne in this land: "I have made a covenant with my chosen; I have sworn unto David my servant; your seed will I establish for ever, and build up your throne to all generations" (Ps 89.4-5); Yahweh, through prophet Nathan, promised David the establishment of his kingdom for ever: "He (son of David) shall build a house for my name, and I will establish the throne of his kingdom for ever" (2Sam 7.13, 16).

After the death of Solomon, this glorious kingdom was divided into two (Israel and Judah), and both became weak and politically dependent on the great emperors for their existence. In 722 B.C., the Northern Kingdom was destroyed by the Assyrians. The same fate met the Southern Kingdom in 586 B.C. The subsequent exile from this Promised Land, the destruction of the temple of Yahweh and the 'eternal' monarchy, appeared to say that the promises of Yahweh were futile (cf. Ps 89.50). At the same time, their destroyers, the Babylonians, seemed to ‘prove’ the power of their national god through their military victories and great national festivals.

With the birth of a new generation in exile, the old foundations of faith were further weakened and the traditional links were broken.[36] The new generation experienced very little about the power of the Judean God; consequently, the transmission of the traditional faith in Yahweh, "a God who had failed before Marduk," became a serious problem. A religious crisis was the natural outcome which was aggravated by the absence of Yahweh for a considerable length of time (cf. Is 42.14).

In this crisis situation that resulted from the long exile, instead of being swept away by the strong religious currents prevalent in Babylon, the religion of the Judean ethnic group developed further and learned to exist even in the absence of temple and monarchy because the exilic

---

[36] For example, Ezra 2.59 speaks about a group who could not even prove their descent.

theologians succeeded in reinterpreting the tradition and faith. This seems to be the critical context in which Second Isaiah reinterpreted the traditional concept of the chosen servant (cf. Is 41.8-9), because in the monarchic Israel this title was primarily applied to the king. We will later come back to this point in the analysis section.

In 562 B.C., Nebuchadnezzar died, and Amel-Marduk (Evil-Merodach) became his successor (562-560 B.C.). The new emperor had compassion on the imprisoned Judean king, Jehoiachin; therefore, he released him from confinement (2King 25.27-30; Jer 52.31-34). Even though the king did not come back to Judah, his release probably raised new hope in the exiles, depicting a time of divine favor. The new emperor, probably after a rebe-llion, was succeeded by Nergal-sharuṣur (Neriglissar) who reigned for four years. His son, who was young, came to power in 556 B.C.

In the same year, Nabonidus of Haran, who was probably a rebel, replaced him and took power.[37] Nabonidus was not from the royal family but was of western Aramean origin; he was really proud of his Assyrian and Chaldean ancestry. After his campaigns in Cilicia (553 B.C.), the emperor left for Syria, Anti-Lebanon, and Arabia. He made the oasis of Tema his principal residence, fortified it, and stationed his troops there;[38] subse-

---

[37] Ackroyd, *Exile and Restoration*, 19. The details of how Nabonidus came to power are unknown; cf. R. H. Sack, "Nabonidus," *ABD* IV, 973

[38] Haran was one of the important commercial centres of the time (Ezek 27.23). Economic motive seems to have driven the emperor to Tema. Records of the Assyrian kings from Tiglath-pileser III (745–727 B.C.) to Esarhaddon (681–669 B.C.) indicate an awareness

quently, he was away from the capital at least for ten years during which his son Belshazzar ruled the kingdom as co-regent.

Religious conflict was the mark of the Nabonidus era. He was a devotee of Sîn (Moon-god) of Haran, and tried to popularize this devotion in the empire, which had traditionally been the land of Marduk.[39] According to the Cyrus Cylinder, the gods were enraged at this act and left the temples.[40] During the time of Nebuchadnezzar, the devotion to Marduk was at its zenith, and the New Year Festival was held in high esteem.[41] During his sojourn in Tema in Arabia, however, Nabonidus neglected this important festival; this action appeared to the people as if

---

of the immense economic resources of Northern Arabia. By 600 B.C. Tema became a major urban centre (Jer 25.23), and controlled the trade of incense (Job 6.19). There the emperor could impose tribute in the form of spices and gold on a number of local tribes; cf. J. Albright, "Haran," *BibIl* 16 (1989), 2-3, 7-10; K. Galling, *Studien zur Geschichte Israels im persischen Zeitalter*, Tübingen, Mohr/Siebeck, 1964, 17-19; Sack, *ABD* IV, 974; "Verse Account of Nabonidus," trans by A. L. Oppenheim, *ANET*, 313-314; .

[39] The Babylonian Chronicles (cf. Oppenheim, *ANET*, 313) accused the emperor of neglecting Marduk and worshipping a new god whom the land had never seen before.

[40] M. Cogan, "Cyrus Cylinder," *COS* II, 315 (lines 9ff.).

[41] During this festival, the universal power of Marduk would impressively be proclaimed; cf. M. Albani, "Deuterojesajas Monotheismus und der babylonische Religionskonflikt und Nabonid," in *Der eine Gott und die Götter*, ed. Oeming, M. and K. Schmid [AThANT 82], Zürich, Theologischer Verlag, 2003, 176; J. Bidmead, *The Akitu Festival* (GDS 2), Piscataway, Gorgias Press, 2002, 3-7, 63-66.

he had turned his back on the kingdom.[42] At the same time, Nabonidus on his part justified his act by saying that his god asked him to ignore this festival for a ten-year period.[43]

Meanwhile, Media grew in power, and became the chief enemy of Babylon. In 559 B.C., Cyrus became the ruler of a Persian tribe in Parsagarda, and a vassal of the king of Anshan. The fortunate and clever Cyrus could unite the whole Persia under him in a short period of time. In 555 B.C., Nabonidus made an alliance with Cyrus against the growing Media. Unexpectedly, Cyrus became the master of Media too because a part of the Median army decided to join him.

In fact, Cyrus' political ambitions were higher than what Nabonidus could perceive. By the time he came back from Tema, Cyrus had already taken advantage of the dissatisfaction of the Babylonians over their king, and presented himself as their redeemer and custodian of true faith. In fact, Cyrus could please both people and the priests wherever he went; he could win much support in Babylon as well. He could obtain favorable oracles from the priests of various traditions, who found him as their liberator, even before he had taken any land. As Cyrus arrived to take over Babylon, one of the generals of Nabonidus joined him and attacked his fellow country-men at Opis near modern Bagdad. In 539 Cyrus' troops entered in Babylon without a significant struggle.

---

[42] Anyone who respected his kingdom, according to the orthodox believers, would have neglected the New Year Festival.

[43] According to Nabonidus, he was only carrying out the orders of Sîn; cf. Oppenheim, *ANET*, 313.

As Cyrus, the great emperor, who usually supported the local populations to maintain their traditional faith, advanced and his conquest of Babylon seemed imminent, Second Isaiah announced the coming of the messiah of Yahweh (cf. Is 44.28; 45.1, 13) for the deliverance of the servant of Yahweh (45.4) that was effected through the hands of the divine warrior: "Yahweh will go out like a mighty man, like a man of war he will stir up his fury... He will show himself mighty against his foes" (Is 42.13); "even the captives of the mighty shall be taken away and the prey of the mighty shall be rescued" (49.25); "Yahweh loved him [Cyrus]; he shall perform his purpose on Babylon, and his arm shall be against the Chaldeans ..." (48.14-15); "I have aroused him in righteousness, and I will make straight all his ways; he *shall build my city and set my exiles free*, not for price or reward, said Yahweh of hosts," 45.13).[44]

In fact, Yahweh's announced plan of the restoration of the temple in Jerusalem fitted with the political strategy of Cyrus who usually enforced the local religious laws and culture as the imperial law, and protected local population from the aggression from their neighboring rulers.[45] Second Isaiah, therefore, called the exiles to go out of Babylon carrying the sacred vessels of Yahweh, which had been carried away by Nebuchadnezzar (Is

---

[44] In Second Isaiah the coming of Cyrus is not presented as a prophecy but as the fulfilment of a prophecy (41.26-27); therefore, the references to Cyrus points to the historical setting of the prophet; cf. Blenkinsopp, *Isaiah 40-55*, 54-55.

[45] Cf. P. R. Bedford, *Temple Restoration in Early Achaemenid Judah* (JSJSup 65), Leiden, Brill, 2001, 132-157.

52.11-12; 2King 25.14).[46] This seems to be the historical-political situation of the pronouncements of Second Isaiah that depicted Yahweh as the great emperor who directed the actions of Cyrus (cf. 40.23; 41.25). In the analysis section, we will come back to this point.

---

[46] Nebuchadnezzar probably placed the captured religious implements or statues in the temple of Marduk in order to symbolize the subjugation of these cities and their gods; cf. Smith-Christopher, "Reassessing," 18.

B. Theological Background of Israel

After having looked at the exilic situation from an external, political, and international point of view, in this part we are going to have a look at the internal theological situation that preceded the exilic religious crisis. This is important because Second Isaiah appears to have reinterpreted the traditional servant of Yahweh concept and linked it with exclusive monotheistic affirmations (cf. 43.10).

Pre-exilic Israel was in general monolatrous because the existence of the gods of the nations did not disturb their religious consciousness.[47] Yahweh was the national

---

[47] There is a problem in accepting an early exclusive worship of Yahweh in Israel because even when revelation is affirmed as the basis of Yahweh worship, the relevant biblical texts do not agree at what point in history this self-revelation of Yahweh actually took place: according to Ex 3.7-15 Yahweh made himself known to Israel for the first time (v 6) by means of a direct revelation to Moses, and subsequently Israel became the people of Yahweh (Ex 19); according to Gen 4.26 the descendents of Seth (antediluvian fathers) worshipped Yahweh; as said by Gen 4.3-4 Cain and Abel brought to Yahweh sacrifices prescribed by the Levitical law. The patriarchs worshipped Yahweh and offered similar sacrifices (Gen 5.29; 9.26; 14.22; 15.2; 18.27; 21.33; 27.20; 28.16; 29.32-35; 31.49); see the detailed discussion on this problem in Dijkstra, "El, the God of Israel," 81-126. Another problem is this: older texts (Ps 68; Hab 3; Deut 32; 33 Judg 5) do not speak about the Exodus of Yahweh from Egypt, or revelation on Sinai and his coming to Zion;

God of Israel, similar to the other ancient Near Eastern national gods who were the gods of the surrounding nations: thus Phoenicians worshipped Baal-Asherah pair, Moabites Chemosh, Ammonites Milcom, Philistines Baalzebub-Asherah pair, Assyrians Assur, and Egyptians Amun-Re. Israel also recognized the existence of these gods as it is clear from the words of the prophet Micah: "For all people will walk every one in the name of his god, and we will walk in the name of Yahweh our God for ever and ever" (4.5).

Non-Israelites were thought to be the people of the foreign gods and they were helped and protected by these gods (cf. 2Chr 25.14-16). This idea was well articulated in the discourse of Jephthah to the king of Ammon: "Will you not inherit what your god Chemosh gives you? Likewise, whatever Yahweh our God made us inherit we will possess" (Judg 11.24).

This monolatrous notion of Yahweh was not an insignificant deviation from the 'true faith' because one can find several biblical texts that present Israel as having a monolatrous faith: Yahweh spoke to Moses to execute judgment on the gods (Ex 12.12; Num 33.4). Joshua asked the people to make a choice between Yahweh and the gods (Josh 24.14-15); David thought that other gods

---

they speak about the march of Yahweh from Seir (Northern Sinai) through Transjordan to Bashan. According to De Moor (*The Rise of Yahwism*, 223-234) the coming of Yahweh from Sinai to Zion (Ex 15) might have been a Davidic innovation in order to justify the earthly kingship. According to Loretz ("Das Ähnen," 499-507) the command to worship only Yahweh (Ex 20.3; Deut 5.7) is probably a command that prohibits idols in the family cults of Israelites (Deut 26.14; Ex 22.19; 23.13).

really existed: "they have driven me out this day from abiding in the inheritance of Yahweh, saying, 'Go, serve other gods'" (1Sam 26.19). According to 2Sam 5.21, when David had victory over the Philistines, he carried off their idols; this story, which appeared improper, was later corrected by the Chronicler (1Chr 14.12).[48] When the Israelite King Ahaziah lay sick, this king sent messengers to Baalzebub, the god of Ekron, in order to know if he would recover (2King 1.2). Passages that speak about the idolatry of the pre-exilic Israel, as interpreted by the Deuteronomist, are not rare in the Bible (1King 11.1-8; 2King 17.29-41).

Again, according to the biblical accounts, Yahweh was not the sole deity who received sacrifices from the population and the kings.[49]

---

[48] See the comments on this text by Cogan, *Imperialism*, 116.

[49] It is true that the majority of the early Israelite personal names with theophoric elements were related to Yahweh or El as authors have suggested; cf. N. Avigad, "The Contribution of Hebrew Seals to an Understanding of Israelite Religion and Society," in *Ancient Israelite Religion*, ed. P. D. Miller, et al., 195-208; J. D. Fowler, *Theophoric Personal Names in Ancient Hebrew* (JSOTSup 49), Sheffield, JSOT, 1988; De Moor, *The Rise of Yahwism*, 10-11; J. H. Tigay, *You Shall Have no Other Gods.* Israelite Religion in the Light of Hebrew Inscriptions (HSS 31), Atlanta, Scholars Press, 1986; "Israelite Religion: The Onomastic and Epigraphic Evidence," in *Ancient Israelite Religion*, ed. P. D. Miller, et al., 157-194. The names alone, however, would not prove the orthodox faith of a society because in most cultures, personal names are related to family traditions and the names of the forefathers. For example, even though Ahab had a Pheonecian wife who was totally dedicated to Baal, their sons bore Yahwist names: Ahaziah (1King 22.51), and Jehoram (2King 1.17).

There are frequent references to Asheroth[50] and to the family gods. Archaeological findings suggests that

[50] The opinion of scholars on Asherah (40 occurrences in 9 biblical books) can be generally divided into two groups: (1) One group thinks that Asherah is only a cult object, either a wooden image, a sanctuary, grove, or living tree; this idea prevailed until the discovery of Ugaritic material; cf. E. Cortese, "I tentativi d'una teologia (Christiana) dell' AT," *LA* 56 (2006), 9-28; A. Lemaire, "Les inscriptions de Khirbet el-Qôm et l'Ashéra de Yhwh," *RB* 84 (1977), 595-608; "Who or What Was Yahweh's Asherah? Startling New Inscriptions from Two Different Sites Reopen the Debate About the Meaning of Asherah," *BAR* 10 (1984), 42-51; E. Lipinski, "The Goddess Atirat in Ancient Arabia, in Babylon, and in Ugarit," *OLP* 3 (1972), 101-119; (2) A second group thinks that Asherah was both the name of a wooden object and the name of a goddess; cf. F. M. Cross, *Canaanite Myth and Hebrew Epic*, Cambridge, Harvard University, 1973; J. Day, "Asherah in the Hebrew Bible and Northwest Semitic Literature," *JBL* 105 (1986), 385-408; W. G. Dever, "Recent Archaeological Confirmation of the Cult of Asherah in Ancient Israel," *HS* 23 (1982), 37-44; J. A. Emerton, "'Yahweh and His Asherah': The Goddess or Her Symbol?," *VT* 49 (1999), 315-337; D. N. Freedman, "Yahweh of Samaria and His Asherah," *BA* 50 (1987), 241-249; J. M. Hadley, "Yahweh and 'His Asherah': Archaeological and Textual Evidence for the Cult of the Goddess," in *Ein Gott allein?* ed. Dietrich and Klopfenstein, 235-37; Z. Meshel, *Kuntillet 'Ajrûd a Religious Centre From the Time of the Judean Monarchy on the Border of Sinai* (IMJC 175), Jerusalem, Israel Museum, 1978; "Did Yahweh Have a Consort?," *BA* 5 (1979), 24-35; S. M. Olyan, *Asherah and the Cult of Yahweh in Israel* (SBLMS 34), Atlanta, Scholars Press, 1988; R. Patai, "The Goddess Asherah," *JNES* 24 (1965), 37-52; M. S. Smith, *The Early History of God.* Yahweh and the other Deities in Ancient Israel, 2nd ed. (BRS), Grand Rapids, Eerdmans, 2002, 47-54.

Israelites believed in Ashera who was thought to be the Mother-Goddess;[51] many of them seem to have worship-

---

[51] Comparative study of biblical texts with Nuzi-texts suggests that the expression ‘our god’ and the texts that prohibit image worship were references to the family gods in Israel (Ex 20.2-3; 22.7-8, 19; 34.14; Deut 5.7-8); cf. Loretz, "Das Ähnen," 495-507. The emergence of Aherah (consort of El) as the consort of Yahweh was the probably an outcome of the equation of Yahweh with El, the head of the Canaanite pantheon; cf. Day, "Asherah in the Hebrew Bible," 385-408. In fact, in recent years, archaeology has been unearthing more and more evidences to extensive pre-exilic devotion to Asherah, the fertility goddess of Canaan: in Ugarit and in Hittite translation of a Canaanite myth, Asherah is the consort of the creator God El; she later merged with Anat and Astart; she is mentioned as a goddess in the Old and Late Babylonian texts. In Egypt (New Kingdom) and in Philistine Ekron, she was worshipped under the name Qadesh; in Phoenicia she was identified with Ashtart; M. C. A. Korpel, "Asherah Outside Israel," in *Only one God?* ed. Becking, B., et al., 2001, 127-150. Most important among these archaeological findings are the ninth-eighth century shrine unearthed in Kuntillet ’Ajrûd (the northern part of Sinai Peninsula), and the Tomb inscription from Khirbet el-Qôm (between Lachish and Hebron). From the theophoric names (+YW), it is concluded that Kuntillet ’Ajrûd was a sanctuary used by the people of the Northern Kingdom, Israel. Here three inscriptions, which seem to be standard formulae, mentioned Yahweh together with his Asherah with topographical connections (Inscription 1: ‘Message of [my] Lord the ki[ng]. Say to Yahl[el] and to Yoasa. [No]w, I have blessed you by Yahweh of Samaria and by his Asherah. Inscription 2: ["Message]of Amaryaw, S/ay to my Lord:/ Is all well with you? I have blessed you by Yahweh of Teman and his Ashera..." Inscription 3: ["I have blessed you] by Yahweh of Teman and his *Ashera*?"). Similarly, a tomb inscription in which Yahweh appears with Asherah was discovered from Khirbet el-Qôm: (["For?] Uriyahu, the wealthy, is this written:

ped Baalim and Asheroth (Judg 3.7; 10.6; 2King 17.16; Hos 11.2; Jer 11.13-17);[52] several kings gave leadership in this devotion (1King 14.14-15, 21-23; 15.9-15; 16.33; 2King 21.3-7); some of them tolerated it (2King 13.6); the righteous kings, Josiah and Hezekiah, tried to destroy it (2King 18.4; 23.6, 14; cf. also 2King 18.19-25). Even if Asheroth were only emblems of Yahweh, it is true that they existed and were destroyed by the reform kings.[53]

'Blessed be Uriyahu by YHWH and more than his enemies by his Asherah - save him" for/by Abi/Oniyahu [..by Y]HW[H] and his Asherah [] his..[..]'"). These translations are from Dijkstra, "I have Blessed," *Only one God?* ed. Becking, B., et al., 2001, 17-44; cf. also W. G. Dever, "Iron Age Epigraphic Material from the Area of Khirbet el-Qôm," *HUCA* 40-41 (1969-70), 139-189; "Ancient Israelite Religion," 112-113, 121-122. Emerton, "New Light on Israelite Religion," 2-20; Hadley, "Some Drawings," 180-213; "The Khirbet el-Qôm Inscription," 50-62; Meshel, *Kuntillet 'Ajrud*; Lemaire, "Les inscriptions," 595-608; U. Winter, *Frau und Göttin* (OBO 53), Freiburg, Vandenhoeck & Ruprecht, 1983, 486-490; S. Schroer, *In Israel gab es Bilder* (OBO 74), Freiburg, Vandenhoeck & Ruprecht, 1987, 30-45. Mono-Yahwism was at least a minority religion in the pre-exilic period. In fact, the Yahwism created and reformed by Deuteronomistic historians had been projected to the past, to the days of Solomon, in order to criticize the present; cf. Day, "Yahweh and the Gods," 184-186; M. S. Smith, "Yahweh and Other Deities in Ancient Israel: Observations on Old Problems and Recent Trents," in *Ein Gott allein?* ed. Dietrich and Klopfenstein, 199-200.

[52] There were of course people who were against these cults: Judg 6.25-27; 1King 15.13.

[53] In fact, several kings had foreign women as their wives who often led them to their gods (e.g., Solomon - 1King 11.1; Rehoboam - 1King 14.21; Ahab - 1King 16.31).

Even in the well known fight for Yahweh by Elijah monotheism is not self-evident (1King 18.17-40). King Ahab introduced the cult of Phoenician national god Baal in Israel which probably brought the traditional national deity, Yahweh, to an inferior position to Baal due to the authority exercised by Ahab's Phoenician Queen Jezebel (1King 16.31-34).[54] As already mentioned, each nation was thought to be the land of its national god,[55] and the important temples were the centers of economy of the time.

Elijah summoned the 450 prophets of Baal and 400 prophets of Asherah[56] on Mount Carmel in order to make

---

[54] Historically speaking, Ahab was a successful king: in his time the economy improved, and co-operation between the kings of the region including Judah, made the region strong against the outside forces; this is ignored by the biblical accounts; cf. J. B. Hennessy, "Excavations at Samaria-Sebaste, 1968," *Levant* 2 (1970), 1-21; L. J. Hoppe, "History of Israel: Monarchic Period," *ABD* III, 564.

[55] El was the head of the Canaanite pantheon in the first millennium; however, each nation had its national patron deity; accordingly, Yahweh was the national deity of Israel; cf. Smith, "Yahweh and Other Deities," 212. This point is confirmed by Deut 32.8 (cf. the English translation of RSV).

[56] Several inscriptions dating from seventh to third century B.C. show that Asherah was known and venerated as a goddess in and around Judah. For example, the three line of a dedicatory inscription discovered in Philistine Ekron reads in the following way: (a) for Asherah, (b) holy for Asherah, (c) holy according to the prescription of Qadshu.' For detailed discussion and bibliography see Dijkstra, "I have blessed," 17-44; since Bible presents Asherah as the companion of Baal and not of El or Yahweh, and no Israelite personal names appear with that of Asherah, and her name is absent from Mesha inscription, Korpel

a decision ‘who the real God was?’ (vv 19-20); subsequently, the prophet challenged the people to make a choice ‘who the real God of Israel was?’ and to declare it (cf. 1King 18.38): Baal or Yahweh? Notably, the people had no answer, probably because they had never made such a hard decision before (v 21; see v 39).

After the unforgettable sacrifice that brought these people to a clear decision in favor of Yahweh, the prophet killed all the 450 prophets of Baal, but did nothing, according to the biblical report, against the 400 prophets of Asherah: probably because she was not a threat to the superior power of Yahweh in the country (v 40).[57] It is true that afterwards the courageous Elijah was horrified by the menace of Jezebel and would flee from her. Similarly, the question that Elijah repeatedly asked Ahaziah and his messengers implied only monolatry: "Is it because there is no God in Israel that you are going to inquire of Baalzebub, the god of Ekron?" (2King 1.3, 6, 16).

The rebellion of Jehu, who was anointed as the king of Israel by the decision of Elisha, overthrew the Omrides and the Baal devotees through a chain of awful human slaughter (2King 9-10); however, Jehu himself did not accept Yahweh as the only God, rather, he worshipped the golden calves in Bethel and Dan (2King 10.29-31). From these points several critical authors conclude that Elijah, Elisha, and Jehu were involved in a reform move-

("Asherah Outside Israel," 145-149) suggests that devotion to Asherah was probably part of the folk religion in Israel.

[57] Psalm 29 that is considered to be one of the oldest songs in the Hebrew Bible, addresses the sons of gods (בְּנֵי אֵלִים, v 1); for the dating of the Psalm cf. W. L. Holladay, *The Psalms through Three Thousand Years*, Minneapolis, Fortress, 1993, 21-23.

ment of nationalistic focus rather than a transformation aimed at a monotheistic change.[58]

This state of affairs continued until the time of King Josiah, exile, and even after (cf. Ps 97.7).[59] Jeremiah lamented: "Your gods have become as many as your towns, O Judah, and as many as the streets of Jerusalem; you have set up the altars to shame, to burn incense to Baal" (11.13). Later, when Jeremiah was taken to Egypt, he met with stiff resistance from the Israelites living there to renounce their traditional faith in the Queen of Heaven (i.e., Asherah[60]) because they actually believed that she had been responsible for their prosperity in Judah (Jer

---

[58] See for example, V. Nikiprowetsky, "Ethical Monotheism," *Daedalus* 104.2 (1975), 68-69; F. Stolz, "Der Monotheismus Israels im Kontext der altorientalischen Religionsgeschichte - Tendenzen neuerer Forschung," in *Ein Gott allein?* ed. Dietrich and Klopfenstein, 33-50; M. Ottosson, "The Prophet Elijah's Visit to Zarephath," in *In the Shelter of Elyon.* Essays on Ancient Palestinian Life and Literature in Honor of G. W. Ahlström (JSOTSup 31), ed. W. B. Barrick, et al., Sheffield, JSOT, 1984, 185-198; G. Hentschel, "Elija und der Kult des Baal," in *Gott, der Einzige.* Zur Entstehung des Monotheismus in Israel (QD 104), ed. E. Haag, Freiburg, Herder, 1985, 54-90; Smith, *The Early History of God*; W. M. Schniedewind, "History and Interpretation: The Religion of Ahab and Manasseh in the Book of Kings," *CBQ* 55 (1993), 649-661; J. Jeremias, "Der Begriff 'Baal' im Hoseabuch und seine Wirkungsgeschichte," in *Hosea und Amos.* Studien zu den Anfängen des Dodekapropheton (FAT 13), Tübingen, Mohr/Siebeck, 1996, 86-103.

[59] About the post-exilic dating of the psalm see H.-J. Kraus, *Die Königsherrschaft Gottes im Alten Testament* (BhT 13), Tübingen, Mohr/Siebeck, 1951, 133-36.

[60] Dijkstra, "El, the God of Israel," 113-120.

44.16-19);[61] moreover, even at the end of the fifth century, a goddess called Anat-Yaho or Anat-Bethel was worshipped in the Elephantine by the Jews.[62]

In addition, even after the exile only those who returned from Babylon to Palestine were convinced of Yahweh as the only God (pro-Yahweh monotheism). Ezekiel speaking about the exiles said: "they (exiles) will come there (back to the land) and will remove from it all its detestable things and all its abominations. And I will give them one heart, and a new spirit I will set within them; I will take the stony heart out of their flesh and give them a heart of flesh, *that they will walk in my statutes and keep my ordinances* (מִשְׁפָּט) and do them; and they shall be my people, and I will be their God" (11.18-20; compare Is 48.4-5: "because I knew that you are obstinate, and your neck an iron sinew and your forehead

---

[61] "As for the word that you have spoken unto us in the name of Yahweh, we are not going to listen to you. But we will do everything that we have vowed, burn incense to the queen of heaven and pour out libations to her, as we did, both we and our fathers, our kings and our princes, in the cities of Judah and in the streets of Jerusalem; for then we had plenty of food, and prospered, and saw no evil. But since we left off burning incense to the queen of heaven and pouring out libations to her, we have lacked everything and have been consumed by the sword and by famine. And when we burned incense to the queen of heaven and poured out libations to her, was it without our husbands' approval that we made cakes for her bearing her image and poured out libations to her?" (Jer 44.16-19).

[62] R. Albertz, *A History of Israelite Religion in the Old Testament Period.* From the Beginnings to the End of the Monarchy, trans by J. Bowden (OTL), London, SCM, 1994, 211. One of the Judges in Israel was called Shamgar ben Anat (Judg 3.31).

brass ... before they came to pass I announced them to you, lest you should say, 'My idol did them, my graven image and my molten image commanded them'").

That pre-exilic Israel was idolatrous is also evident from the community of Jews and Aramaeans of the military colony of Elephantine who had a temple dedicated to the Queen of Heaven.[63] In the background of the practice of the biblical authors to retroject their theology into the distant past in order to legitimize the present by depicting a particular picture in the past,[64] the discovered elements from Elephantine are also important to understand the pre-exilic Israelite religion. According to the prophet Micah, Israel had to go to Babylon in order to be redeemed: "In that day, word of Yahweh, I will assemble the lame and gather those who have been driven away, and those whom I have afflicted, and the lame I will make the remnant, and those who were cast off, a strong nation, and Yahweh will reign over them in Mount Zion *from this time forth and for ever*" (4.6-7).[65]

Exilic and post exilic literatures, by contrast, have a clearer monotheistic conception. Second Isaiah is in fact the most important biblical author who discusses the motif of monotheism; this shows the important role that he played in the history of the development of Israelite

---

[63] A letter addressing an inhabitant of the island reads in the following way: "Greetings to the temple of Bethel and the temple of the Queen of Heaven...."; cf. B. Porten, ed. *Jews of Elephantine and Arameans of Syene.* Aramaic Texts with Translation, Jerusalem, Hebrew University, 1974, 159 (4,1).

[64] J. Blenkinsopp, *Ezra-Nehemiah* (OTL), London, SCM, 1989, 41-47.

[65] Cf. Deut 30.1-8; Ezek 11.18-20; Jer 30.3, 9, 22.

monotheism. As mentioned above, he also reinterpreted the traditional servant of Yahweh concept in relation to pro-Yahweh monotheism (cf. 43.10). Here emerges the need of investigating the relationship between the servant concept and Isaianic monotheism.

This theological setting may be further clarified if we take a look into the origin and development of the Yahweh-alone movement that seems to have led Israel from monolatry to monotheism.

The Yahweh-Alone Movement

As mentioned above, the pre-exilic Israel in general had a monolatrous notion of their God; the post-exilic Israel by contrast has a monotheistic notion of the same God; therefore, what really happened in exile is an important question to be answered. Was this shift from monolatry to monotheism an exilic revolutionary change or was it an evolutionary change? It seems that it was a growth that already began in the prophetic circles of the pre-exilic Israel which later flowered in exile. The history of the development of monotheism in Israel may be outlined in the following way.

After the military coup of Jehu and before the appearance of the prophet Hosea (around 750 B.C.), there probably emerged a religious movement in the Northern Kingdom which scholars label as 'the Yahweh-alone movement.'[66] This new religious movement emphasized

---

[66] The idea of a Yahweh-alone party/movement was first proposed by M. Smith, *Palestinian Parties and Politics that Shaped the Old Testament*, 2nd corr. ed. London, SCM, 1987, 17, 29; then it has

the faith in Yahweh based on their tradition of the exodus-redemption and the prophetic word. The Book of Hosea is the main document from which one knows about this new faction.

Hosea announced the following words of Yahweh: "and I, Yahweh, am your God ever since the land of Egypt; you will not know any God beside me and besides me there is no savior" (13.4; see also 12.10-11). Hosea, who in a religious context of the existence of several high places announced that Yahweh desire *love* and not sacrifice, *knowledge of God* rather than burnt offerings (Hos 6.6), seems to have laid the ground work for the later exclusive monotheism.

Many people at that time continued to be polytheistic offering sacrifices to Baalim and Asheroth (Hos 3.1; 2.13,

---

been followed by a number of authors under the leadership of B. Lang (*Monotheism*, 33-35; "Die Jahwe-allein-Bewegung," in *Der eine Gott und die Götter*, 97-110); cf. also R. Albertz, "Der Ort des Monotheismus," in *Ein Gott allein?* ed. Dietrich and Klopfenstein, 77-96; Dever, "Ancient Israelite," 105-125; W. Dietrich, "Überwerden und Wesen des Biblischen Monotheismus: Religiongeschichtliche und theologische Perspektiven," in *Ein Gott allein?* ed. Dietrich and Klopfenstein, 13-30; "Der Eine Gott als Symbol politischen Wiederstands. Religion und Politik im Judah des 7. Jahrhunderts," in *Ein Gott allein?* ed. Dietrich and Klopfenstein, 463-490; R. K. Gnuse, *No Other Gods*. Emergent Monotheism in Israel (JSOTSup 241), Sheffield, 1997 202-203; W. H. Schmidt, "Monotheismus: Altes Testament," *TRE* 23, 237-248; G. Theissen, *Biblical Faith*, trans by J. Bowden, Philadelphia, Fortress, 1985; M. Weippert, "Synkretismus und Monotheismus: Religionsinterne Konfliktbewaeltigung im alten Israel," in *Kultur und Konflikt*, ed. Assmann, J. and D. Harth (ESNF 612), Frankfurt, Suhrkamp, 1990, 143-179.

2.17; 11.2). Hosea believed that the lack of knowledge and true love of God were the basic problems on the way of true faith (4.6). He, therefore, spoke strongly against the popular beliefs by employing the covenant metaphor; he totally dedicated his life, first by marrying a prostitute (1.2-8), and then by buying an adulterous woman -- even though she had another lover (3.1-5) -- in order to demonstrate to the Israelites the seriousness of their idolatry (2.4-15; 4.10-19; 5.3-4; 6.10; 7.4; 8.4-5; 9.1, 10; 10.5; 11.2; 13.1-3; 14.9). For him Jerusalem was the only right religious centre: "Ephraim has surrounded me with lies, and the house of Israel with deceit, but Judah still walks with God..." (11.12; see also 4.12-14; 8.5-6; 10.5; 1King 12.25-33). Even though the zealous Judean prophet Amos was his contemporary and spoke mainly to the people of the north, he was not concerned with this problem which was so vital for Hosea. Also Isaiah and Micah were not different from Amos; therefore, the new move (of Hosea) might be seen as an insignificant faction in the Israelite society.

The Sargon Inscription documented that gods *in whom Israel trusted* were transported to Assyria by the Emperor (722 B.C.). This suggests that the official religion (of the kings) of the Northern Kingdom was not aniconic.[67]

---

[67] The Sargon Prism lines 32-33 read the following: "and the gods of their confidence as spoil I counted." This unusual phrase does not seem to be literary topos but refers to an actual event; moreover, these were images of gods and not simple *maṣṣēbôt* (standing stones); cf. B. Becking, "The Gods, in Whom They Trusted...: Assyrian Evidence for Iconic Polytheism in Ancient Israel," in *Only one God?* ed. Becking, B., et al., 2001, 151-163; C. J. Gadd, "Inscribed Prisms of Sargon II from Nimrud," *Iraq* 16 (1954), 173-

When, thus, the Northern Kingdom fell, the Yahweh-alone party probably came to the Southern Kingdom.[68] The humiliation of the Northern Kingdom, which had idols in the official religion, probably became an opportunity to the Yahweh-alone party to interpret this downfall as the result of the false worship and as the

---

201, re-edited A. Fuchs, *Die Inschriften Sargons II aus Khorsabad*, Göttingen, Cuvillier, 1993, 82-188, 313-342. According to N. Na'aman (*Ancient Israel's History and Historiography*, Winona Lake, Eisenbrauns, 2006, 311-338) although in Judah Yahweh was represented through standing stones (*maṣṣēbôt*), in Israel images of Yahweh existed. At the same time T. N. D. Mettinger ("Aniconism - A West Semitic Context for the Israelite Phenomenon," in *Ein Gott allein?* ed. Dietrich and Klopfenstein, 159-178) observes that the idea of aiconism was present in some of the Semitic cultures: Arabic, Nabatean, Phoenician, Egyptian and Mesopotamian. If this is so, the so-called Israelite aniconism was part of the common culture and cannot be mixed with the modern idea of aniconism based on monotheism.

[68] From Jer 41.4-5, one can assume that when Northern Kingdom fell, those northerners who were faithful to Jerusalem came to the south. According to 2Chr 30.1-11, 18, Hezekiah invited all the northerners, that escaped from the Assyrian deportation, to celebrate the Passover in Jerusalem. Bible also gives Psalms and other traditions originated in the north: see, for example, Ps 80 (the geographical descriptions); Ps 10 (employs northern dialect - בַּל - similar to Phoenician and Ugaritic), and Ps 45 (the reference to Tyre and description of a palace which seems to be that in Samaria). For other texts that come from north see Holladay, *The Psalms*, 27-28. That the northern population came to the south seems to be confirmed by archaeological data as well; cf. M. Broshi, "Estimating the Population of Ancient Jerusalem," *BAR* 4 (1978), 10-15.

consequence of not following the teaching of Hosea (2King 17.5-18; Ps 78.9-11[69]).

King Hezekiah, who struggled to survive politically and militarily, seems to have accepted this teaching to a certain extent;[70] subsequently, he destroyed many cultic objects and removed the bronze serpent (an old Yahweh symbol) from the temple (2King 18.3-4, 22; 2Chr 31.1). The arrival of Sennacherib to Jerusalem (701 B.C.), and the miraculous redemption of the Holy City seems to have strengthened the movement (2King 18.13-37; see v 32; 19.8-13, 35-37).[71] During the reign of Manasseh, however, the idolatrous practices returned to Judah and the temple in Jerusalem: "the graven image of Asherah that he had made, he (Manasseh) set in the house of ... Yahweh ..." (2King 21.2-9; 23.26).[72]

The movement then makes itself visible in the Josianic reform (641-609 B.C.) which authors label as a reform in

---

[69] For comments about the psalm see E. Haglund, *Historical Motifs in the Psalms* (CBOT 23), Lund, CWK Gleerup, 1984, 89.

[70] According to L. K. Handy ("Hezekiah's Unlikely Reform," *ZAW* 100 [1988], 111-115), even Hezekiah was not a monotheist: he removed the sanctuaries outside Jerusalem only to protect the statues of gods from the Assyrian military. By destroying the local cultic places, Hezekiah probably wanted to prevent Assyrians from making offering to the god of the country in the local sanctuaries and thus winning local support; cf. M. Weinfeld, "Cult Centralization in Israel," *JNES* 23 (1964), 204. These studies point to the uncertainity of the historical value of the biblical accounts about Hezekiah.

[71] Actually, Hezekiah was challenged by Rabshakeh because he had destroyed the altars of Yahweh throughout Judah (2King 18.22).

[72] Mendenhall, *Ancient Israel*, 161-166.

the direction of monotheism that declared the exclusive worship of Yahweh. On a certain day, the high priest of the temple, Hilkiah, brought to the king a scroll which they had 'found' during the restoration work (2King 22.11).[73] After having read this scroll, according to the Deuteronomistic historian, the king did a thorough purification work of religion and temple (2King 23.1-25): he removed all idolatrous priests and vessels of Baalim from the temple of Jerusalem; he closed all shrines of Baalim and Asheroth outside Jerusalem[74] and made them impure

---

[73] Scholars have suggested, as Lang ("Die Jahwe-allein-Bewegung," 101-103) groups them, four possible interpretations to this mysterious 'finding': (a) According to St Jerome, this was the Book of Deuteronomy (cf. his comment on 2King 22.8). Several modern authors identify this as Deut 12-26. (b) According to J. R. Lundbom ("The Lawbook of the Josianic Reform," *CBQ* 38 [1976], 293-302), Hilkiah in fact found a book in the temple which must have contained Deut 32. (c) According to E. Otto (*Das Deuteronomium.* Politische Theologie und Rechtsreform in Juda und Assyrien [BZAW 284], Berlin, Gruyter, 1999), Hilkiah found a hidden book that contained a good portion of Deuteronomy: the book was written by the Yahweh-alone party (of two or three generations before Josiah), who employed the same language of Esarhaddon's vassal treaty in order to fight against that emperor. Since the king of the time was not favorable these fighters had to disappear for a while hiding the book in the temple. (d) According to Lang (*Monotheism*, 39), Hilkiah did not find the book but he wrote the book which contained the two main mottoes of Yahweh-alone party (see next page). In fact, these diverging opinions of the scholars converge in a particular point: they all agree that the book (found) was a portion of Deuteronomic Work, the author of which was actually a Yahweh-alonist.

[74] Archaeology discovered a number of Israelite temples and altars from this region: at Dan, Megiddo, Ta'anach, Tell el-Far'ach,

with the bones of the dead; he burned the great Asherah image that was in the temple; he removed male prostitutes from there; he destroyed high places of sacrifice throughout the country; he destroyed the Topheth where Israelites used sacrifice their children to Molech in the Hinnom valley; he removed the horses dedicated to the sun and burned their chariots; he destroyed the altars of sun (cf. Ezek 8.16); he destroyed Solomon's old shrines, and shattered the shrines at Samaria and Bethel. The contemporary prophet Zephaniah seems to have been an adherent of the movement (cf. Zeph 1.4-6).

The Josianic move was probably the beginning of the radical breakthrough to monotheism.[75] At this point the movement had two important objectives: the centralization of cult of Yahweh in Jerusalem, and the purification of cult. With the possibility to control the cult in Jerusalem, the movement seems to have reached its objective to a certain level; however, when Josiah -- the champion of Yahweh-alone party -- was killed by Neco in 609 B.C., Yahweh-alonists, who appeared to be the

---

Lachish, Arad, and probably also in Beersheva; for a summary treatment on these cultic centers cf. Dever, "Ancient Israelite," 108-110; A. Biran, ed. *Temples and high places in Biblical times.* Proceedings of the Colloquium in Honor of the Centennial of Hebrew Union College-Jewish Institut of Religion. Jerusalem 14-16 March 1977, Jerusalem, N. Glück School of Biblical Archaeology of Hebrew Union College-Jewish Institut, 1981. Josephus (*Ant*, 11.7-8) and Mishna (*Menahoth*, 11.10) speak about the existence of an Israelite temple in Leontopolis, in Egypt; there was a Jewish temple in Elephantine before the coming of Cambyses; cf. R. de Vaux, *Ancient Israel.* Its Life and Institutions, trans by J. McHugh (BRS), Grand Rapids, Eerdmans, 1997, 341-343.

[75] Cf. Gnuse, *No Other Gods*, 204.

protagonists of a deluded hope, seems to have lost the control over the cult (cf. 2Chr 35.23-25; Lam 3); accordingly, images of gods returned to the temple (Ezek 8; 2King 23.37).

Prophet Ezekiel and Jeremiah were adherents of this movement (Jer 44.1-7; 8.14; 9.13-14; 23.15 cf. Num 5.11-31) and prepared way for the breakthrough of monotheism in exile. In fact, by interpreting history and judging his ancestors as idolatrous, Deuteronomist historian communicated that pre-exilic Israelite religion was not (exclusively) monotheistic.[76]

In 586 B.C. Judah was destroyed. This made two contrasting interpretations of the history possible: for one group of the people, the destruction was the result of stopping their devotion to Asherah and similar other popular pious practices related to the local sanctuaries (cf. 2King 18.22);[77] according to the Yahweh-alone party, by

---

[76] A. de Pury, "Erwaegungen zu einem vorexilischen Staemmejahwismus: Hos 12 und die Auseinandersetzung um die Identitaet Israels und seines Gottes," in *Ein Gott allein?* ed. Dietrich and Klopfenstein, 414-15; Gnuse, *No Other Gods*, 205; Schniedewind, "History and Interpretation," 649-661.

[77] As mentioned above (cf. foot note 62), after the destruction of Judah, Jeremiah met the Jews in Egypt and told them that the disaster was the result of their idolatry (Jer 44.1-15). The people then with stern intention of continuing their worship of Asherah contradicted Jeremiah and told him that they would do everything according to their tradition because when they used to offer sacrifices and drink offerings to the Queen of Heaven, they had enough bread and well being; since the time when they stopped that worship, probably referring to the Josianic reform, they had been lacking in everything (Jer 44.16-18). People probably could not accept Jeremiah's view because according to the ancient Near

contrast, this destruction was the result of the idolatry of Judah,[78] viz., they were punished to worship other gods: "Yahweh will bring you, and your king whom you will set over you, to a nation that neither you nor your fathers have known; and there you shall serve other gods of wood and stone" (Deut 28.36, 64; also Deut 4.25-27; Jer 16.13).[79]

Deuteronomistic History,[80] Jeremiah, Ezekiel, and Second Isaiah were the important documents of Yahweh-alone party that came from this period; following Hosea, they interpreted the idolatry of Israel in terms of infidelity in a conjugal relationship (Hos 1.2; Jer 2.20-25, 32-37; 3.1-14; 31.31-32; Ezek 16; 23; Is 50.1-3).[81]

Eastern thought, religious renovations by kings had to be approved by the relevant deities; a political failure, therefore, meant the wrath of these gods; cf. T. H. Robinson, *A History of Israel*. From the Exodus to the Fall of Jerusalem, 586 B.C., Oxford, Clarendon, 1932, 403; Weinfeld, "Cult Centralization," 209.

78 2King 24.3; 21.10-16; Deut 31.16-17; Is 42.24-25; 43.27-28; 50.1; Jer 5.19; 9.13; 7.18; 15.4; 16.11; 25.1-14; 37.6-40.5; 44.2-6; Lam 2.1-10; 4.11-16; Ezek 8.1-9.2; 43.6-8.

79 Cf. 2King 21.10-25; destruction of Samaria 2King 17.1-23 (see especially vv 7-8); Is 42.24-25; Jer 44.1-15; Ezek 16; 20; 23; 6.3; 20.28.

80 Deuteronomist couldn't see meny good things in Israel's past seven centuries of history (so also Is 48 and Ezek 20). He reformulated the law with clearer monotheistic emphasis and put it in the mouth of Moses (4.35, 39; 32.29).

81 The Yahweh-alone movement seems to have founded Judaism as a pure monotheistic religion by means of six approaches: (1) its adherents conceived their task as a God-given mission to destroy idolatry and build up real faith (Jer 1.4-19 [cf. vv 5, 10, 16]; Ezek 3.1-11 [cf. vv 4-5, 8]; 21.1-4; Is 40.4-5, 9-10; 41.14-16; 49.1-2;

It is therefore conceivable that the Yahweh-alone party in exile had a mixed audience to address: 1) the elite adherents of the movement, who considered themselves as the true/elected Israel, who could accept Yahweh as the supreme God without difficulty (Jer 24.1-7; 29.16-23; Ezek 11.14-21; 33.24-29; Is 49.1-6; 50.4-9); 2) the others who considered Yahweh as a powerless God who was unable to bring them prosperity (Ezek 37.11; Is 40.27; 50.2). The presence of the latter is clear because Second Isaiah often summoned nations and their gods/idols into trial in order to demonstrate their inability: "Set forth your case, Yahweh is saying; bring your proofs, the King of Jacob is saying" (41.21-26; 43.8-13; 44.6-8). If his audience did not believe in the existence of these gods, such a mode of prophetic ministry would have been inapt.

50.7-9); (2) they emphasized the importance of the written word of God (Deut 9.10; 17.18-19; Josh 1.8; 8.34; 23.26; 1King 2.3; 2King 14.6; 2King 22; 28.58-59; 29.20, 27; 30.10; Hos 8.12; Jer 30.2; 36; Ezek 2.1-3.11; 43.11-12; Is 40.8); (3) they emphasized the role of education and knowledge of the law of Yahweh (Hos 4.1, 6; 5.4; 6.6; Jer 3.15; 10.14[= 51.17]; 14.18; 5.5-8; Deut 4.6; 5.6-7; 6.20-25; 17.18-19; 31.9-13; Is 44.19; 45.20; 50.4-5); (4) they interpreted Sabbath as the day of complete worship of Yahweh (Deut 5.12-15; Jer 17.19-27; Ezek 46.1-12; Neh 13.15-22); (5) they established orthodox control over prophecy (Jer 28.9; Ezek 13.1-6; 14.9-12; Deut 13.2-6, 9; 18.22; Is 40.8) and marriage (Deut 7.1-4; Ezra 10.6-44); and (6) they announced the restoration of Jewish state with Jerusalem as its centre (Jer 31.1-6, 10-12; 50; Ezek 43.6-9; Deut 30.1-10; Is 45.14). The new temple dedicated in 515 B.C. after exile was thus completely monotheistic and Yahweh-alone party became the leading movement of Judaism (cf. Ezra 9-10); even then the Jews in Elephantine seem to have continued to be polytheists; cf. also the comments of Lang on the Yahweh-alone party, *Monotheism and the Prophetic Minority*, 41-44.

This seems to be the theological background of Second Isaiah who presented Yahweh as the only God having universal authority, and Israel as his chosen mandate (49.5-6).[82]

In exile the faithful Yahweh-alone party wanted to revive the traditional faith and make people return to their ancestral land (Jer 3.15-18). It therefore tried to reinterpret the traditional concepts that appeared to be meaningless and tried to present religious responsibility as personal. For example, according to the traditional doctrine, every disaster that happened to Israel was the result of the transgression of their fathers: "... Our fathers sinned, and are no more; and we bear their iniquities" (cf. Lam 5.6-7; Ex 20.5); God would punish them, they thought, for the transgression of their fathers.

This point was clearly articulated in the traditional notion of faith as it was revealed to Moses: "Yahweh passed before him (Moses), and proclaimed, 'Yahweh, Yahweh, a merciful God and gracious, slow to anger, and abounding in steadfast love and faithfulness, keeping

---

[82] There are a number of authors who already analyzed the theme of monotheism in Second Isaiah; most of them come to the conclusion that Isaianic monotheism was the answer to the exilic crisis in the Israelite religion; cf. Albani, "Deuterojesajas Monotheismus," 171-201; H. Klein, "Der Beweis der Einzigkeit Jahwes bei Deuterojesaja," *VT* 35 (1985), 267-73; M. C. Lind, "Monotheism, Power and Justice: A Study in Second Isaiah," *CBQ* 46 (1984), 432-46; Loretz, "Das Ähnen," 491-527; M. S. Smith, "Monotheism in Isaiah 40-55," in *The Origins of Biblical Monotheism*, New York, Oxford University, 2001, 179-194, 298-302; C. H. Tobias, "Monotheism in Isaiah 40-55", Baptist Theological Seminary PhD diss., New Orleans, 1982; Vorländer, "Der Monotheismus," 84-113; Wildberger, "Der Monotheismus," 49-273.

steadfast love for thousands, forgiving iniquity and transgression and sin, but who will by no means clear the guilty, visiting the iniquity of the fathers upon the children and the children's children, to the third and the fourth generation." (Ex 34.6-7; cf. also Ex 20.5-6; Num 14.18; Deut 5.9-10; 2Sam 21.1-14; 24.15-16).

In exile, this belief actually led the community into a serious fatalistic attitude -- a religious crisis; then, the Yahweh-alone party tried to emphasize the individual responsibility of the believer before Yahweh; it totally abandoned the 'kingdom' (monarchical) language and the hearers were addressed as the 'house of Jacob,' the 'house of Israel,' and the 'house of Judah.' Jeremiah, for example, wrote: "In those days they shall no longer say 'fathers have eaten sour grapes, and the children's teeth will be set on edge'; but every one shall die for his own sin; each man who eats sour grapes, his teeth shall be set on edge" (31.29-30).

Similarly, Ezekiel declared: "What do you mean by repeating this proverb concerning the land of Israel, 'fathers will eat sour grapes, and the children's teeth will be set on edge'? ... This proverb shall no more be used by you in Israel; behold, all souls are mine; the soul of the father as well as the soul of the son is mine: the soul that sins shall die" (18.2-4; cf. also 3.16-21; 18.19; 33.18-19). The author of Deuteronomy wrote: "Fathers shall not be put to death for their children, nor shall the children be put to death for their fathers; every man shall be put to death for his own sin" (24.16).

The exilic poet-prophet Second Isaiah seems to have expressed this new theological vision in a colorful language, i.e., by means of his 'servant of Yahweh' ideal.

Exile was thought to be the result of the transgression of the kings and leaders of Israel against Yahweh (cf. 2King 21.10-15); in the context of the destroyed religious and political institutions, including the dynasty which had received the promise of an eternal throne (Ps 89.4), Second Isaiah seems to have democratized[83] the royal servant of Yahweh concept (41.8-9); by reinterpreting this traditional concept he rendered all the Israelites responsible for their present state of life: "Who gave up Jacob (the servant) to the spoiler...? Was it not Yahweh, against whom *we have sinned*, in whose ways they would not walk, and whose law they did not obey?" (Is 42.19, 24). His monotheism gave him the theological setting to declare this new interpretation.

At the same time, these exilic theologians also tried to shed light on the problem of the innocent people undergoing suffering. As suggested by Mendenhall, the person of Job (in the Book of Job) tries to answer an important exilic question: what is the point in continuing the worship of Yahweh? The question is set in the mouth of the wife of Job: "then his wife said to him (Job), 'Do you still hold fast your integrity? Curse God, and die.'" (Job 2.9). Why should Job, the righteous, suffer? Has Yahweh failed him? Based on the conventional views, the three friends of Job argue that Job should repent because no righteous man will have to undergo suffering. Job, who is

[83] The word democratization here does not imply the modern idea of the rule of the people. It only means that a title that was usually applied to certain chosen individuals in the pre-exilic Israel was now applied to the people as a whole.

not willing to abandon Yahweh, personifies the faithful Judean community in exile.

Even though the three friends demand from Job a return (repent) to the established traditions in order to have a future, Job rejects that view; instead, he demands a face-to-face explanation from Yahweh for his suffering. At the end Yahweh comes before Job not to give such an explanation but only to show his magnificence and to deny the arguments of the three friends. It is then revealed to the friends of Job that his suffering is the will of Yahweh and it is the suffering of a righteous man.

The book comes to the conclusion that the future of the community does not depend on the established religious slogans and traditions; it rather consists in a dynamic encounter with God and the acceptance of the unquestionable greatness of Yahweh as Job did: "My ears had heard of you but now my eyes have seen you; therefore, I will despise myself and repent in dust and ashes" (Job 42.5-6).[84]

The story of Job tries to say that Job is innocent but he is suffering according to a divine plan for which he has been chosen as the servant of Yahweh: "Yahweh said to Satan: 'Have you considered *my servant* Job, that there is none like him on the earth, a blameless and upright man, who fears God and turns away from evil?'" (Job 1.8, 22; 2.1, 3). In fact, he appears to be similar to the innocent Isaianic servant (Is 53.9), who, according to the plan of Yahweh undergoes severe affliction (Job 1.12; 2.6; Is

---

[84] Mendenhall, *Ancient Israel*, 189-190; Tharekadavil, "How Great is This Life That You Have Given Me O Lord," *Indian Journal of Family Studies* 2 (2006), 5-15.

50.7; 53.10). The bystanders considered both these servants -- Job and Isaianic servant -- as smitten by God (Job 8.20; 53.3-4). Both these servants attain future through the faithful submission to the will of Yahweh (Job 42.10-17; Is 53.10b-12). Both are servants of Yahweh chosen to teach their fellow exiles a new religious truth (Job 42.7; Is 42.4; 49.1-6; 50.4; 53.11), and both intercede for them (Job 42.8-9; Is 53.12). The Isaianic servant is the Israel in whom Yahweh will be glorified (Is 49.3; compare Job 42.7). Both these servant figures seem to originate from schools with comparable theological principles. If this is true, in the exilic period any faithful person similar to Job could be labeled as the servant of Yahweh; this label then indicated that the person referred to was able to undergo any humiliation or suffering for the sake of the plan of Yahweh that would unveil a new future for the believers (Is 42.4a; 50.6; 53.8).

One can conclude by saying that from the time of Hosea the ancient Israelite religion was constantly undergoing a development in the direction of exclusive monotheism and it found a very significant breakthrough in exile as the result of the efforts and vision of the Yahweh-alone party. Second Isaiah is the most important biblical author who seriously discusses the motif of monotheism. Isaianic servant of Yahweh concept is also linked with his monotheistic affirmations; therefore it should be analyzed in the context of this theological development that took place in the Israelite religion.

C. Theological Setting in Mesopotamia

After having looked at the inner theological development in the pre-exilic and exilic Israelite religion we are now going to have a short look at the external (Babylonian) theological factors that seems to have influenced the Isaianic servant of Yahweh concept. This is important because Second Isaiah lived in Babylon and his message reflects the Babylonian setting (cf. 40.18-20; 44.9-20; 46.1).

The Babylonian society in which the Judean exiles lived and Second Isaiah taught was of a multi-theological nature. From the time of Nebuchadnezzar, Marduk had been exalted as the supreme god and Marduk-theology dominated the scene; later Sîn-theology of Nabonidus, on its part, exalted Sîn as the supreme god; the military victories of Cyrus probably pictured Ahura Mazda as the most powerful god. Surprisingly, all these three theological currents were moving in the direction of monotheism.[85]

Towards the end of the second millennium, Marduk absorbed and displaced all the other Babylonian gods and

[85] This monotheistic tendency was not totally new. The Assyrian concept of god had monotheistic nuances; cf. S. Parpola, *Assyrian Prophecies* (SAA 9), Helsinki, University Press, 1997, XXI.

ruled as the supreme-god for a time.[86] In the Marduk-theology, in fact, there was a growing tendency to develop into a monotheistic system. In reality, *Enûma Elish*, a document composed in the beginning of the first millennium, revealed a growing inclination towards monotheism.[87]

In this literary work, that was recited in the Babylonian New Year Festival, at least six monotheistic nuances were evident: (a) it announced the absolute kingship of Marduk over gods, (b) Marduk was given 50 names, that

---

[86] W. G. Lambert ("The Historical Development of the Mesopotamian Pantheon: A Study in Sophisticated Polytheism," in *Unity & Diversity*. Essays in the History, Literature, and Religion of the Ancient Near East, ed. Goedicke, H. and J. J. M. Roberts [JHNES 7], Baltimore, Johns Hopkins University, 1975, 191-200, 197-199) reproduces a document (CT 24 50, BM 47406, obverse) that shows how Marduk had absorbed all the important gods of Mesopotamian pantheon: Urash (is) Marduk of planting, Lugalidda (is) Marduk of the abyss, Ninurta (is) Marduk of the pickaxe, Nergal (is) Marduk of battle, Zababa (is) Marduk of warfare, Enlil (is) Marduk of lordship and consultations, Nabû (is) Marduk of accounting, Sîn (is) Marduk who lights up the night, Šamaš (is) Marduk of justice, Adad (is) Marduk of rain, Tišpak (is) Marduk of troops, Great Anu (is) Marduk of…, Šuqamuna (is) Marduk of the container, … (is) Marduk of everything. Only the goddesses and demons might have been left aside: the last lines of the document are missing. This, according to Lambert, can be qualified as monotheism because some of the Christian churches professed monotheism even when they believed in the supernatural personal evil; cf. also Albani, "Deuterojesajas Monotheismus," 182-183.

[87] According to T. Abusch, ("Marduk," *DDD*, 1022-23), this epic was composed during a period of Babylon's weakness when the interest of temple and palace coalesced in order to reaffirm the city's claim to cultural heritage.

were the names of the important Mesopotamian gods, through which all these gods lost their personal identity and became part of Marduk's hypostasis,[88] (c) through this exaltation, the earlier idea of the assembly of gods was replaced,[89] (d) after the fight with Tiâmat, Marduk had became the creator of the world, (e) being the warrior and redeemer-god, he got the authority to determine the destinies of other gods and stars, and (f) Marduk became the incomparable god (VI, 102, 106, 121-129). This tendency to eliminate the powers of the Babylonian gods by Marduk-theology and the idea of the incomparability of Marduk presented in *Enûma Elish* were, in fact, developments in the direction of monotheism.[90]

Marduk-theology announced that the destruction of Babylon by Sennacherib (689 B.C.), and the exile of the Marduk statue were not due to the powerlessness of Marduk; rather they were due to his anger over Babylon

---

[88] The last part of the *Enûma Elish* gives fifty names to Marduk: fifty is the number of Enlil's gods. Marduk had become the god of gods, sun of gods (VI, 127). The idea is also found in other texts; therefore, some scholars see this tendency as a growth to inclusive monotheism in which other gods were integrated in Marduk and thus became the centre of cosmic powers, while some others reject this idea. For discussion see Albani, "Deuterojesajas Monotheismus," 183-84; B. Hartmann, "Monotheismus in Mesopotamien?," in *Monotheismus im Alten Israel und seiner Umwelt* (BiBt 14), ed. O. Keel, et al., Fribourg, Schweizerisches Katholische Bibelwerk, 1980, 49-81; Parpola, *Assyrian prophecies*, XXI-XXVI; Vuk, "Religione Nazione," 115-128; F. Stolz, *Einführung in den biblischen Monotheismus,* Darmstadt, Wissenschaftliche Buchgesellschaft, 1996, 53; van der Toorn, "God," *DDD*, 678.

[89] Abusch, *DDD*, 1020.

[90] Albani, "Deuterojesajas Monotheismus," 184-85.

as the result of their sin. The Babylonian god would punish them for a period of seventy years.[91] The idea is similar to several oracles of the prophets of Yahweh. Prophet Jeremiah for example spoke of a seventy-year-period exile of the people of Yahweh (Jer 25.11; 29.10).

At the same time, with the ascension of Nabonidus the throne of Babylonian empire, there was a progressive propensity to exalt Sîn as the only and supreme God.[92] In order to demonstrate this point, Paul Alain Beaulieu, even though he himself qualifies Nabonidus as a fanatic, brings arguments from the building inscriptions of Nabonidus. He divides the credibly dated building inscriptions of Nabonidus into three groups according to the three phases of the emperor's life: the inscriptions which were written before his departure to Arabian Peninsula (Inscription no 1, 2, 5, 6), the inscriptions written during his stay in the oasis of Tema (Inscription, 7, 8, 9, 11, 10), and those written after his return to Babylon (Inscription, 13, 14, 15, 16, 17).[93] These inscriptions show the emperor's devotion to Sîn and explain his attempts to establish a Sîn-oriented monotheism.

---

[91] Three inscriptions -- Marduk prophecy, Esarhaddon Inscription, and Babel Stele -- depicted the destruction of Babylon as the result of Marduk's anger. This is comparable to the biblical idea about the destruction of Judah in 587 B.C. (Is 42.24); cf. Albani, "Deuterojesajas Monotheismus," 178-179, esp. footnote no 38.

[92] This attempt, however, did not succeed probably due to two reasons: (1) the opposition from the Marduk-priests, and (2) the early downfall of the reign of Nabonidus (17 years).

[93] For the catalogue, chronology, and bibliography of these inscriptions cf. Beaulieu, *The Reign of Nabonidus King of Babylon 556-539 B.C.* (YNER 10), New Haven, Yale University, 1989, 20-42.

In the first group of inscriptions, Marduk is exalted as the highest god. In these texts, the name of Sîn appears together with other gods. Also in the second group of inscriptions, Marduk is exalted as the supreme god, and Sîn appears only once (Inscription 10). By contrast, in the third group of inscriptions occurs a sharp change: surprisingly, all the inscriptions in this group are related to Sîn-Shamash-Ishtar and to the daughter of Sîn. Sîn is constantly exalted while Marduk is virtually ignored except in one inscription (15) in which he is only a companion of Sîn.

In the last inscription (17), Sîn is the only god mentioned by name; here Nabonidus addresses Sîn in plural ('gods', king of gods), which is similar to the name of the Hebrew God (*ᵉlōhîm*); Sîn is qualified as 'lord of gods of heaven and the netherworld having universal authority,' 'king of the gods,' 'gods of the gods who dwells in great heavens,' and 'the lord of Ur,' (these are actually the titles of Marduk); the temples of Marduk and Nabû in Esagil and Ezida are now declared to be the dwellings of Sîn; Nabonidus prays to Sîn to save him and his son from sinning against that deity -- both in heart and in cultic matters; thus, in this inscription, Sîn, displacing all others, gains prominence and becomes the supreme and only god.[94]

---

[94] It was Sîn who aroused Sennacherib, king of Assyria, to destroy the temple in Eulmaš of Sippar-Anunītum and lay the city in ruins (Inscription 16d, col III, 26-29); the destruction of the city and temple in Ehulhul, that used to be attributed to the anger of Marduk (Inscription I, col II, 1-20), are now attributed to the anger of Sîn (Inscription 15, col I, 11-13); this is the same with the command to rebuild it; gods obey Sîn's orders (col III, 33); Sîn calls rulers to

One can see indications of these Babylonian monotheistic religious trends in Second Isaiah. In Is 47, for example, Yahweh accuses Babylon/Chaldea for her claims to be the only one who is in control of everything: "who say in your heart, I am, and there is no one besides me" (v 8; comp. 45.21, אֲנִי יְהוָה וְאֵין עוֹד); "you said in your heart, I am, and there is no other" (v 10b; compare with 45.22, אֲנִי אֵל וְאֵין עוֹד). In Second Isaiah the expression "I am, and there is no other" is usually a monotheistic affirmation of Yahweh (cf. 43.11; 45.5-6, 14, 18, 21). The Babylonian claims as quoted by Second Isaiah show that Second Isaiah was facing a religious society that began to think in terms of monotheism, even though it had no refined and exclusive monotheistic theology.

Similar to the abovementioned Babylonian religious currents, the Persian religion also became an important external element that helped to shape the Isaianic thought. Cyrus, the Persian, was the victor and hero of the time. He, however, was neither a devotee of Marduk, nor of Sîn, nor of Yahweh: he was a Persian with his own religious background. As the religion of the conqueror, Persian Zoroastrianism became the third theological

---

kingship; Nabonidus has been called by Sîn from his mothers womb (Inscription 15, col I, 4-5); Sin is addressed as the 'lord of lords,' 'king of kings,' 'lord of the gods,' 'king of the gods'; all these titles and attributes given to Sîn show that Sîn-theology was thinking of Sîn as the universal god; cf. Beaulieu, *The Reign of Nabonidus*, 61-62; "Nabunidus' Rebuilding of E-LUGAL-GALGA-SISA The Ziggurat of Ur (2.123B)," *COS* 2 (2000), 313-14; H. J. W. Drijvers, *Cults and Beliefs at Edessa* (EPROR 82), Leiden, Brill, 1980, 122-145; M. Stol, "Sîn," *DDD*, 1480-81.

current that possibly set the background of the message of Second Isaiah.[95]

The Persian theological influence on Second Isaiah can be retained due to three reasons: (a) Zoroastrianism had an earlier origin,[96] (b) it considered Ahura Mazda as the creator of the world and humankind (compare Is 45.12: "I, Yahweh, made the earth, and created man upon it; I, my hands stretched out the heavens, and I commanded all their host"),[97] and (c) according to Persian dualism,

---

[95] Authors dispute whether Zoroastrianism was monotheistic or dualistic. It is taken as monotheistic because Yasna 32.3-5, reads in the following way: "But you gods all are a manifestation of evil thinking, and he who so much worships you [is a manifestation] of falsehood and dissent." This religion can also be considered as a dualism because it believes in the existence of two spirits: Ahura Mazda (God) and Angra Mainyu (evil spirit). It can therefore be called a qualified monotheism; making a more specific definition seems to be difficult; cf. M. Boyce, *A History of Zoroastrianism.* The Early Period (HO 1, 8, 1, 2, 2A, 1); *A History of Zoroastrianism.* Under the Achaemenians (HO 1, 8, 1, 2, 2A, 2), Leiden, Brill, 1975, 1982; "Zoroaster, Zoroastrianism," *ABD* VI, 1170; Vorländer, "Der Monotheismus," 84-113; Lang, *Monotheism*, 47-48; M. Smith, "II Isaiah and the Persians," in *Studies in the Cult of Yahweh*, ed. Cohen, S. J. D. and M. Smith (RGRW 130), Leiden, Brill, 1996," 73-84; E. M. Yamauchi, *Persia and the Bible*, Grand Rapids, Baker, 1996, 137, 422-424, 437-438.

[96] N. Cohn (*Cosmos Chaos and the World to Come.* The Ancient Roots of Apocalyptic Faith, New Haven, Yale University, 1993, 77-81) dates the time of Zoroaster between 1500-1200 B.C. and discusses the influence of Zoroastrianism on the Jews.

[97] According to Yasna 44.3-7 Ahuramazda is the creator of sun, moon, stars, plants, light, darkness, morning, noon, and night; accoring to Bundahishn 1.23-28; 25.1-2, the world was created in six stages; in the final stage man was created.

Ahriman was responsible for the creation of evil that is revealed in darkness, night, winter, draught, infertile land, vermin, sickness, and death. Second Isaiah seems to be aware of this Persian thought (cf. Is 45.6-7: "I am Yahweh, and there is none [beside me]; who *forms light and creates darkness, makes weal and creates woe*, I am Yahweh who do all these things").

The religion of the victor, who respected the local customs, must have influenced those people who were conquered by them;[98] in this situation, in order to safeguard the traditional faith, it was necessary then to go beyond the theological difficulties created by the Persian religious thought. By affirming Yahweh as the one who does everything (creator of both good and evil) and by making Yahweh's claims on Cyrus, the prophet tried to present Yahweh as the only God. The emphatic affirmation of the prophet in 46.12-13 shows that Second Isaiah was announcing the imminent restoration of Zion: "Hearken to me, you stubborn of heart, you who are far away from deliverance: I have brought near my deliverance, it is not far off, and my salvation will not tarry; I will grant salvation in Zion, to Israel my glory" (see also 44.28; 45.13).

One can therefore say that in the exilic period, there was a general tendency in the important religions in Babylon to think philosophically about their main gods

---

[98] Usually the god of the victor absorbed the god of those who were conquered; cf. van der Toorn, *DDD*, 677. It is also true that the biblical authors never condemn the Persian rulers; still, there was the need of affirming the divinity of Yahweh in order to help the people to hold on to their traditional faith.

and to exalt them as the only and supreme deities. The victorious emperors were seen as the earthly messengers of these gods. In that society, a rhetoric based on a monolatrous notion of a god had little space especially because in the eyes of many of the exiles Yahweh was a 'failed' God. Announcement of pro-Yahweh monotheism was really a need of the time. If all the religions around him thought in terms of monotheism, the prophet could not do otherwise if at all to get any attention. In this context, as a faithful follower of his religion, Second Isaiah was internally compelled to announce his God as the only God with universal authority (cf. 45.5-6, 22). Isaianic notion of the call of Israel to be the servant / mandate of Yahweh (the only God) should therefore be set in this general theological setting.

D. Conclusion

Isaiah 40-53 gives indications to conclude that the message was announced to the exiles in Babylon. An understanding of the conceptual background of the exiles in Babylonian thus seems to be helpful to understand the depth of the Isaianic message. Even though Yahweh had promised a land and an eternal monarchy to the Israelites, great emperors of the time destroyed the kingdoms of Yahweh. The subsequent exile of the people of Yahweh depicted his promises as futile. This led the religion into a crisis which was aggravated by some of the traditional beliefs.

Exilic theologians tried to overcome this problem by reinterpreting the traditional faith. The Isaianic concept of the servant of Yahweh seems to be one of such reinterpretations: in this critical historical setting the prophet depicted Yahweh as the greatest emperor and Israel as his servant. In fact, in the pre-exilic Israel, only certain chosen people could be labeled as the servant of Yahweh.

According to the ancient Near Eastern thinking, wars, victories, and failures of kings on earth were only reflections of what was going on in the heavens in the realm of the gods. In the exilic setting of the people of Yahweh in which the imperial powers presented their gods as universal and all powerful, no monolatrous theology of the traditional deity would be strong enough to convince the people of the power of Yahweh. At this crucial and critical moment, Second Isaiah seems to have come up with his well reflected monotheistic theology. Isaiah's notion of the servant of Yahweh is obviously linked with this theology of monotheism.

Notably, ancient Israelite religion had only a monolatrous notion of God. From the time of prophet Hosea, however, an internal move in the religion was trying to affirm an exclusive monotheism. This movement found its mature expression in Second Isaiah. Actually, the exilic period was a historical time in which monotheistic thought was becoming familiar in Babylonian religions. It is therefore necessary to look into the relationship between monotheism and the servant concept.

II

Analysis of Relevant Texts

As mentioned in the foregoing section, in the eyes of the exiles, the great emperors who acted as if the earthly agents of their gods were the supreme powers who directed the history. As a result, the image of the emperor was the best and the most powerful image to speak about the power of the only God. So Second Isaiah seems to have depicted Yahweh as the universal emperor whose power was insuperable; Israel was then presented as the servant and earthly mandate of this emperor. This metaphor appears to be the key to understand the Isaianic concept of the servant.

The following pages will therefore discuss all the important Isaianic texts that present Yahweh as the universal ruler-emperor and all the texts that discuss the motif of the servant of Yahweh. In fact, most of these texts also present the motif of the regeneration of Israel as the servant/mandate; this point will also be given due importance.

In the translation given below, more relevant clauses and themes will be highlighted in italics.

1) 40.9-11

9 עַל הַר־גָּבֹהַ עֲלִי־לָךְ מְבַשֶּׂרֶת צִיּוֹן
הָרִימִי בַכֹּחַ קוֹלֵךְ מְבַשֶּׂרֶת יְרוּשָׁלָםִ
הָרִימִי אַל־תִּירָאִי אִמְרִי לְעָרֵי יְהוּדָה
הִנֵּה אֱלֹהֵיכֶם
10 הִנֵּה אֲדֹנָי יְהוִה בְּחָזָק יָבוֹא וּזְרֹעוֹ מֹשְׁלָה לוֹ
הִנֵּה שְׂכָרוֹ אִתּוֹ וּפְעֻלָּתוֹ לְפָנָיו
11 כְּרֹעֶה עֶדְרוֹ יִרְעֶה בִּזְרֹעוֹ יְקַבֵּץ טְלָאִים
וּבְחֵיקוֹ יִשָּׂא עָלוֹת יְנַהֵל

[9] Get you up to a high mountain, O Zion's herald of good tidings;

lift up your voice with strength, O Jerusalem's herald of good tidings,

lift (it) up, fear not; say to the cities of Judah,

"Behold your God!"

[10] Behold, *the Lord Yahweh will come with might, and his arm rules for him*;

Behold, his reward is with him, and his recompense before him.

[11] *Like a shepherd,* he will feed his flock; in his arms he will gather the lambs,

and will carry them in his bosom, he will lead those that are with young.

This is the last part of the so-called prologue of Second Isaiah (40.1-11). In this text, a herald of Zion is commanded to announce a message.[99] The text has the form of an instruction to a victory herald (cf. 1Sam 31.9; 2Sam 1.20; 18.19-21), a genre that comes from the secular and military realm; the imperative of the verb say (*'imrî*, אִמְרִי) and the demonstrative particle *hinnēh* (הִנֵּה) belong to this genre.[100] The reference to the ruling arm of Yahweh ("his arm rules for him," v 10) and the literary context that speaks about a military service of the people ("her warfare is ended," 40.2) confirm this point. In the present verses the herald is commanded to go up the mountain and declare that Yahweh is coming to Zion as a mighty and victorious ruler (v 10); he will be a shepherd for his people. Notably, in the ancient Near East the image of a shepherd was commonly used for gods and kings even from the 3rd Millennium.[101]

---

[99] The question 'who is the messenger (מְבַשֶּׂרֶת, feminine participle)?' is not clear from the text; therefore, some translators (ESV, KJV, NAB, NAS, NRSV, RSV) count Zion-Jerusalem as appositions to מְבַשֶּׂרֶת (this interpretation is also supported by the following imperative feminine singular verbs), while others (ASV, BBE, LXE, NIB, NIV) consider it as genitive in the absolute state (מְבַשֶּׂרֶת יְרוּשָׁלִָם; מְבַשֶּׂרֶת צִיּוֹן), i.e., מְבַשֶּׂרֶת is a herald sent to Zion. This problem, however, is resolved by another similar text (Is 52.7) which undoubtedly separates Zion from the herald: there the herald is specified as one who announces the good news to Zion. In fact, in Hebrew the feminine participle can be used as a masculine singular referring to an office (cf. *Gesenius-Kautzsch-Cowley*, § 122r). For example, in Ecclesiastes 1.1 the author, son of David, entitles himself as קֹהֶלֶת (feminine participle of קהל), or in Ezra one of Solomon's servants is called הַסֹּפֶרֶת (ספר).

[100] Cf. K. Elliger, *Deuterojesaja* (BKAT 11/1), Neukirchen-Vluyn, Neukirchener Verlag, 1978, 33.

[101] J. W. Vancil, "Sheep, Shepherd," *ABD* V, 1187-1190.

2) Is 40.21-24

21 הֲלוֹא תֵדְעוּ הֲלוֹא תִשְׁמָעוּ הֲלוֹא הֻגַּד מֵרֹאשׁ לָכֶם
הֲלוֹא הֲבִינֹתֶם מוֹסְדוֹת הָאָרֶץ
22 הַיֹּשֵׁב עַל־חוּג הָאָרֶץ וְיֹשְׁבֶיהָ כַּחֲגָבִים
הַנּוֹטֶה כַדֹּק שָׁמַיִם וַיִּמְתָּחֵם כָּאֹהֶל לָשָׁבֶת
23 הַנּוֹתֵן רוֹזְנִים לְאָיִן שֹׁפְטֵי אֶרֶץ כַּתֹּהוּ עָשָׂה
24 אַף בַּל־נִטָּעוּ אַף בַּל־זֹרָעוּ אַף בַּל־שֹׁרֵשׁ בָּאָרֶץ
גִּזְעָם וְגַם־נָשַׁף בָּהֶם וַיִּבָשׁוּ וּסְעָרָה כַּקַּשׁ תִּשָּׂאֵם

21 Do you not known? Will you not hear? Has it not been told you from the beginning?

Have you not understood from the foundations of the earth?

22 (It is) *he who sits above the circle of the earth*, and its inhabitants are like grasshoppers;

who stretches out heavens like a curtain, and spreads them out like a tent to dwell in;

23 *who brings princes to nought, and makes the rulers of the earth as nothing.*

24 Scarcely are they planted, scarcely sown, scarcely has their stem taken root in the earth,

he will have blown upon them, and they are already dried up, and they are carried off like stubble by the tempest.

The military figure of Yahweh envisaged in the first text (40.9-11) finds a more developed exposition in the present one. According to these verses, Yahweh is not only a mighty ruler but his kingdom and power supersedes all the earthly empires: his rule is not limited by space and time. Yahweh sits not on an earthly throne; rather, he is seated on the circle of the earth under which the inhabitants of the earth move like grasshoppers that take birth and die in a short time.

Through this metaphor the prophet communicates two points: 1) Yahweh is an everlasting and universal king while the mighty earthly rulers are only like grasshoppers that are limited both by space and time; Yahweh's rule transcends both. 2) These earthly kings are unable to get victory over this great ruler; in fact, even before they are well planted, they are destroyed by Yahweh (v 24). It is he who destroys the princes of the earth (v 23). Israel had already heard about this God from the very beginning (v 21); they had heard this in the pre-exilic period (cf. Is 10.5-6).

Actually, this image of Yahweh is presented as part of a poem that discusses the motif of the incomparability of Yahweh to the nations and their idols/gods (40.12-31; see especially vv 15, 18-20). Yahweh, the great ruler, is not comparable to any of these.

3) 41.1-4, 25

הַחֲרִישׁוּ אֵלַי אִיִּים וּלְאֻמִּים יַחֲלִיפוּ כֹחַ 1
יִגְּשׁוּ אָז יְדַבֵּרוּ יַחְדָּו לַמִּשְׁפָּט נִקְרָבָה
מִי הֵעִיר מִמִּזְרָח צֶדֶק יִקְרָאֵהוּ לְרַגְלוֹ 2
יִתֵּן לְפָנָיו גּוֹיִם וּמְלָכִים יַרְדְּ
יִתֵּן כֶּעָפָר חַרְבּוֹ כְּקַשׁ נִדָּף קַשְׁתּוֹ
יִרְדְּפֵם יַעֲבוֹר שָׁלוֹם אֹרַח בְּרַגְלָיו לֹא יָבוֹא 3
מִי־פָעַל וְעָשָׂה קֹרֵא הַדֹּרוֹת מֵרֹאשׁ 4
אֲנִי יְהוָה רִאשׁוֹן וְאֶת־אַחֲרֹנִים אֲנִי־הוּא

....

25 הַעִירוֹתִי מִצָּפוֹן וַיַּאת מִמִּזְרַח־שֶׁמֶשׁ יִקְרָא בִשְׁמִי
וְיָבֹא סְגָנִים כְּמוֹ־חֹמֶר וּכְמוֹ יוֹצֵר יִרְמָס־טִיט

1 Listen to me in silence, O coastlands; let the peoples renew their strength;
Let them come forward and speak; let us together draw near for judgment (*mišpāt*).
2 *Who stirred up one from the east whom victory* (*ṣedeq*) *meets at every step?*
He will give up nations before him, and on the kings he will have dominion;
He will make them like dust with his sword, like driven stubble with his bow.
3 He pursues them and passes on safely, by paths his feet have not trod.
4 Who has performed and done this, calling the generations from the beginning?
I, am Yahweh, the first, and with the last; I am He.

....

25 *I (Yahweh) stirred up one* from the north, and he has come from the rising of the sun; he shall call on my name in order to come (*weyiqtol*[102]) on *rulers as on mortar*, as the potter treads clay.

These verses are part of a long poem that has the form of a trial scene (41.1-42.4);[103] they link the already presented image of the emperor with concrete history by

---

[102] The reference here is to the Hebrew verbal system presented by A. Niccacci, *The Syntax of the Verb in Classical Hebrew Prose*, trans by W. G. E. Watson (JSOTSup 86), Sheffield, JSOT, 1990.
[103] Cf. Tharekadavil, "Monotheism," 105-114.

announcing that the victorious king Cyrus is brought by Yahweh.[104] In the ancient Near Eastern religious setting one can think about the claims that the Babylonian god Marduk and the god of Cyrus had already asserted on this great emperor (cf. Cyrus cylinder). These claims were apparently reasonable as well.

---

[104] The person referred to in the question 'who raised from the east 'him whom victory (*ṣedeq*) meets…?' refers to Cyrus because the text fits better with the qualifications of Cyrus than anyone else (neither Abraham nor the servant) in Second Isaiah. It is Cyrus who comes from the east, called by Yahweh (41.2, 25; 46.11; 45.6); his coming is related to *ṣedeq* (41.2; 45.13); Yahweh calls him by name (41.25; 45.3); kings and isles are subdued by him (41.2; 45.1, 13); he comes to restore Judah (44.28; 45.4, 13). Jewish tradition (Targum and Rashi) identified the man with Abraham (cf. R. A. J. Rosenberg, ed. *The Book of Isaiah.* A New English Translation, 2nd ed. New York, Judaica Press, 1989, 325). Even though Jewish exegete Ibn Ezra rejected this interpretation, C. C. Torrey (*The Second Isaiah*, New York, Charles Scribner's Sons, 1928, 310-316) still defended this view. J. D. Smart (*History and Theology in Second Isaiah*, Philadelphia, Westminster, 1965, 68-69), on his part, gives the text (41.2) a Christological interpretation. Remarkably, according to Jewish tradition, Abraham's righteousness (*ṣedāqâ*) was related to his *faith* in Yahweh (cf. Gen 15.6); however, in Second Isaiah, *ṣedeq* does not refer to 'righteousness' or faith; it is rather a synonym of redemption (45.8; 51.6, 8; see also verses 1, 5). In 45.13 the prophet says: "I have raised him (Cyrus) up in *ṣedeq* (redemption), and I will make straight all his ways: he shall build my city and he shall let go my captives." Cyrus's *ṣedeq* is related to his military power against the kings and nations -- a power supported by Yahweh (41.2-3). In the context of Is 40-53, therefore, the arguments to identify 'the man from the east' with Abraham does not gain strength against the identification of him with Cyrus.

Yahweh then came up with a question on the guiding force of Cyrus: 'Who stirred up one from the east under whose power all the earthly kings would be made as stubble?' (v 1). This question is followed by an idol-passage that tries to depict the gods as human-made objects (41.5-7); subsequently, Yahweh asserts his absolute claim on Cyrus: "I stirred up one from … the rising of the sun … in order to come on rulers as on mortar, as the potter treads clay" (v 25). Yahweh is the one who directs Cyrus and thus destroys the rulers and kings.

These verses concretely explain the abovementioned two points. (a) In the previous text Yahweh alluded to his everlasting rule by saying that he is sitting on the circle of the earth even from the very beginning of the foundations of the world (40.21); in the present text this point is clearly stated by means of an absolute assertion: "I am Yahweh, the first, and with the last, I am He" (41.4). (b) In the previous text Yahweh said that it is he who brings the princess and rulers to nothingness; they will be carried away like dust by the wind; in the present one he clarifies this point by saying that he now does this concretely through Cyrus ("I stirred up… he will make them like dust with his sword," v 25). Isaianic logic seems to be the following: if Yahweh is the universal emperor whose authority transcends both time and space, Cyrus whose dominion is limited both by time and space can only be under the control of Yahweh.

4) 41.8-9

וְאַתָּה יִשְׂרָאֵל עַבְדִּי 8

יַעֲקֹב אֲשֶׁר בְּחַרְתִּיךָ זֶרַע אַבְרָהָם אֹהֲבִי

9 אֲשֶׁר הֶחֱזַקְתִּיךָ מִקְצוֹת הָאָרֶץ וּמֵאֲצִילֶיהָ קְרָאתִיךָ
וָאֹמַר לְךָ עַבְדִּי־אַתָּה בְּחַרְתִּיךָ וְלֹא מְאַסְתִּיךָ

[8] But you, Israel, are *my servant*, Jacob,
whom I have chosen, the offspring of Abraham, my friend,
[9] (you) whom I took from the ends of the earth, and from its farthest corners called you,
saying to you, You are *my servant*; I have chosen you and did not cast you off.

After presenting Yahweh as the universal and ever living emperor, the prophet turns to the exiles calling them 'the servant of Yahweh.' In Second Isaiah, the noun servant (*'ebed*) appears first in the present text and thus it is the first Isaianic servant passage. In fact, this text defines who the Isaianic servant of Yahweh is, viz., Jacob-Israel, the offspring of Abraham. In this very first servant text, Jacob-Israel, who are gathered from the corners of the earth, are repeatedly told that they are the *chosen servant of Yahweh.*

The servanthood of Israel consists in an election ("You are my servan*t*; I have chosen you"). This might have been a new religious thought proposed to Israel because in the pre-exilic Israel, only the king or other specially elected leaders of the people were labeled as the chosen servant of Yahweh.

For example, the title was applied to the patriarchs, who received the promises of a multitude of descendants and the possession of the land for ever (Ex 32.13; Deut 9.27); the title was applied to Moses (Josh 1.7, 13; 2King 18.12; 20.6; Ps 105.6; Num 12.7), to Caleb (Num 14.24), and to Joshua (Josh 24.29; Judg 2.8) in relation to the exodus from Egypt and the possession of the Promised Land; it was applied to the prophets to whom Yahweh assigned special tasks to carry out (Moses, cf. Deut 34.10; Elijah, 2King 9.36; 10.10; Isaiah, Is 20.3; Jonah, 2King 14.25). The title was also applied to the kings of Israel (David, 2King 19.34; 20.6; Ps 105.6; 42; Eliakim, Is 22.20; Hezekiah, 2Chr 32.16, and Zerubabbel, Hag 2.23). This demands a research into the chosen servant concept in the pre-exilic Israelite religion.

After analyzing the chosen servant concept of the Bible, H. Wildberger concludes that in pre-exilic Israel the concept of election (בחר) was first and foremost linked to the election of the king. For example: "David said to Michal, 'it was before Yahweh, who chose me rather than your father or anyone from his house to appoint me prince over the people of Yahweh, people Israel; I will make merry before Yahweh'" (2Sam 6.21; cf. also 1Sam 10.24; 2Sam 16.18; 2Sam 21.6; 1King 11.13, 32; 2King 19.34; 20.6). The chosen servant was clearly different from his people (1King 8.29-30, 52, 66).

Royal Psalms also combined the election of David with the concept of the servant: "He chose David his servant, and took him from the sheepfolds" (Ps 78.70); "I have made a covenant with my chosen, I have sworn unto David my servant" (89.3; see also v 20).[105] In the last text,

---

[105] Also in Babylon, the king, and not the people, was considered to be the chosen representative of gods on earth. For example, god Ningirsu in his pure heart had chosen Gudea, king of Lagash, as his representative; similarly, Nebuchadnezzar will often be called the chosen one of his god.

election is also seen as an everlasting covenant between Yahweh and the servant: "I will establish your seed for ever, and build up your throne to all generations" (Ps 89.4; reconfirmed in vv 21, 36).

This chosen servant, king, was endowed with the spirit of Yahweh: "and the spirit of God shall rest upon him, the spirit of wisdom and understanding, the spirit of counsel and strength, the spirit of knowledge and of the fear of Yahweh" (Is 11.2).

Through election, David became the servant and representative of Yahweh: "He chose David as his servant ... to be the shepherd of Jacob his people and Israel his inheritance" (Ps 78.70-71; see also 2.6-9). Since Yahweh is faithful (Ps 89.2), this eternal covenant and election could not be cancelled. When Judah was destroyed, and there was no king, in fact, many thought that Yahweh had rejected this covenant (Ps 89.38-45); therefore, Second Isaiah had to reinterpret the concept of the chosen servant; he did it by democratizing the idea and linking it with the election and promise of Yahweh with Abraham (not with David): in this new vision, Israel became the chosen servant of Yahweh and his representative to the world.[106]

This research of Wildberger spots three important points related to the Isaianic idea of the chosen servant of Yahweh: (1) in the pre-exilic Israel the king (David) was first and foremost considered as the chosen servant; (2)

---

[106] H. Wildberger, "Die Neuinterpretation des Erwählungsglaubens Israels in der Krise der Exilszeit: Überlegungen zum Gebrauch von בָּחַר," in *Jahwe und sein Volk* (TBAT 66), ed. H. H. Schmid and O.H. Steck, München, Kaiser, 1979, 193-205.

this election was thought to be an eternal covenant between Yahweh and the monarchy; (3) Second Isaiah democratized the concept of the chosen servant.

The significance of this concept -- of the eternal election of the (royal) servant -- in the tradition of Israel is confirmed by the other exilic prophets, Ezekiel and Jeremiah. For example, Ezekiel says the following: "They shall dwell in the land ... wherein your fathers have dwelt... they, and their children, and their children's children for ever, and David my servant (shall be) their prince for ever" (37.25). Jeremiah expressed it in another way: "If you can break my covenant of the day, and my covenant of the night, and that there should not be day and night in their season, then may also my covenant with David my servant be broken, that he should not have a son to reign upon his throne..." (33.20-21).

Comprehensively then, when the monarchy was overthrown and the exile of the people lasted for a long time, this 'eternal covenant concept' brought the religion into a crisis (cf. Lam 5.20) and it questioned the credibility of the promises of Yahweh. Without doubt, there arose the need of a reinterpretation of the traditional faith in order to make it still acceptable to the faithful and to give a new orientation towards the future.[107] This seems to be the situation in which Second Isaiah presented the exilic Israel as the chosen servant of Yahweh, with an accompanying declaration that Yahweh has not rejected them (v 9).

---

[107] History proves that the Jewish religion was able to survive this religious crisis.

The democratization of the concept of the servant also takes place from an ancient Near Eastern point of view. According to the Babylonian thinking, for example, kingship was thought to have come from heaven and the kings derived their authority through a divine election.[108] The usual relationship that existed between the kings and gods was that of the servant and master; thus Sargon II, Assurnasirpal, and Nebuchadnezzar II were known as servants of their gods.[109] Similarly, in Ugarit King Keret was called *'bd il* (KART A, 150-160).[110] These kings were the mandates and representatives of their gods on the earth.

Second Isaiah seems to have adopted this ancient Near Eastern metaphor in order to reinterpret the traditional chosen servant concept. He applied this metaphor to Israel in the context of the ancient political conceptions.

In the ancient Near East the emperors were labeled as the 'lords' and their vassals were labeled as the 'servants.' The relationship that existed between these two (lord-servant) was that of a covenant. Through these covenants, these suzerains (lords) demanded unconditional faithfulness and obedience from their vassals; they also supported and protected those who were obedient. In the treaties between the emperor and the vassal, the lord-servant lan-

---

[108] Frankfort, *Kingship*, 243.

[109] M.-J. Seux, *Epithètes royales akkadiennes et sumériennes*, Paris, Letouzey et Ané, 1967, 362; T. Jacobsen, *The Treasures of Darkness.* A History of Mesopotamian Religion, New Haven, Yale University, 1976, 158, 160. Jeremiah 43.10 names Nebuchadnezzar, king of Babylon, as the servant of Yahweh.

[110] "Ugaritic Myths, Epics and Legends," trans by H. L. Ginsberg, *ANET* 129-155.

guage, which was interchangeable with father-son, was employed:[111] King Ahab was thus the servant / vassal and son of Tiglath-pileser (2King 16.7-9); Hoshea was the servant/vassal of Shalmaneser (2King 17.3), and Jehoiakim the servant / vassal of Nebuchadnezzar (2King 24.1).[112] The positive comment of the Deuteronomistic historian on Hezekiah was that he did not serve the Assyrian Emperor (2King 18.7; cf. also 2Sam 8.2, 6; 1King 4.21; Ps 18.43; 72.11; Jer 25.11;27.7-17; 28.14; Gen 14.4; 1Chr 18.2, 6; Judg 3.8, 14; 9.28).

Actually, the history of Israel and Judah had convincingly taught these deportees -- that still underwent the consequences of the defeat of their monarchy -- that the stability of the small kingdoms depended heavily on their faithfulness to the great warrior-emperors of the time.[113] Second Isaiah seems to take this reality as a basis to reinterpret the 'chosen servant of Yahweh' concept: he therefore presented Yahweh as an emperor and Israel as his vassal.

The figure of the emperor, who dominated the political and religious scene, was the best imaginable and inte-

---

[111] An Aramaic inscription describes the vassal King Barrakib of Sam'al as a servant of Tiglath-pileser; see H. Donner, *Kanaanäische und aramäische Inschriften* II, Wiesbaden, Otto Harrassowitz, 1964, no. 216, 1-3; 217.1-2; F. C. Fensham, "Father and Son as Terminology for Treaty and Covenant," in *Near Eastern Studies in Honor of William Foxel Albright*, ed. H. Goedicke, Baltimore, 1971, 125; P. Kalluveettil, *Declaration and Covenant* (AnBib 88), Rome, PIB, 1982, 93-99.

[112] In Chronicler's opinion (2Chr 12.8), Israel had to make a choice between serving Yahweh and serving the emperors of the world.

[113] Cogan, *Imperialism*, 2.

lligible earthly image that could express the universal power of Yahweh, the only God. In practice, it was the will of the imperial power and the faithfulness to him that decided the course of the events (cf. 2Chr 28.23).[114] Second Isaiah, therefore, presented Yahweh (the king of Israel, 41.21; 43.15; 44.6; 52.7; 40.10) as the mighty warrior-emperor who brought kings and princes to power, and who helped or destroyed them (40.23; 41.2-4, 15-16, 25; 42.13, 24-25; 43.5-6, 13, 16-17, 27-28; 45.1-3, 13; 48.15; 49.24-25; 50.2; 51.5, 9-10, 15, 22-23); he visualized an international scene in which the kings and princess obeyed Yahweh's commands (43.5-7; 49.22-23), knelt before Yahweh, and sworn allegiance to him (45.23).

Now Yahweh has chosen Israel as his servant (vassal; cf. 49.23). The application of the metaphor is clear because in Second Isaiah Israel is presented not only as the servant of Yahweh, but is also as the son of Yahweh (43.6). As seen above, the vassals were also called the sons of the emperors. This rhetoric of reinterpretation was thus comprehensible to the exilic Israel. At the same time

---

[114] For example, Ahaz was subject to Assyria, and thus saved the kingdom from destruction (cf. 2King 16.3); Hezekiah who organized rebellion had lost 46 walled cities and had to pay a heavy tribute to Assyria (2King 18.13-16); Josiah -- hailed as a reformer -- had died in the Battle against the Egyptians making a historical change in the history of Judah's international relations (2King 23.28-34); Manasse, though heavily accused of idolatry by the Biblical authors, ruled Judah for 55 years because he remained subject to Assyria (2King 21.3); even though the territory was limited, under him Judah thrived more than before; cf. Cogan, *Imperialism*, 66-75, 95; Lipschits, *The Fall*, 360-361.

the application of this metaphor demanded from the exiles a renewed faithfulness to this great emperor (Yahweh); unfaithfulness would bring disaster (48.22). In fact, it was due to their disobedience to their lords (emperors), that Judean monarch (servant) was eliminated from throne.

We can therefore say that in exile Second Isaiah reinterpreted the traditional chosen servant of Yahweh concept by connecting it with the ancient Near Eastern political notion of the lord-servant.

5) 42.1-4

הֵן עַבְדִּי אֶתְמָךְ־בּוֹ בְּחִירִי רָצְתָה נַפְשִׁי 1
נָתַתִּי רוּחִי עָלָיו מִשְׁפָּט לַגּוֹיִם יוֹצִיא
לֹא יִצְעַק וְלֹא יִשָּׂא וְלֹא־יַשְׁמִיעַ בַּחוּץ קוֹלוֹ 2
קָנֶה רָצוּץ לֹא יִשְׁבּוֹר וּפִשְׁתָּה כֵהָה לֹא יְכַבֶּנָּה 3
לֶאֱמֶת יוֹצִיא מִשְׁפָּט
לֹא יִכְהֶה וְלֹא יָרוּץ עַד־יָשִׂים בָּאָרֶץ מִשְׁפָּט 4
וּלְתוֹרָתוֹ אִיִּים יְיַחֵילוּ

1 Behold my servant, whom I will uphold, my chosen, the delight of my soul;
I will have put my Spirit upon him; he will bring forth *mišpāt* to the nations.
2 He will not cry or lift up his voice, or make it heard in the street;
3 A bruised reed he will not break, and a dimly burning wick he will not quench;
He will faithfully bring forth *mišpāt*.
4 He will not fail or be discouraged till he establishes *mišpāt*

on the earth;
and the coastlands will wait for his teaching (*tôrāh*).

According to the Israelite tradition, the persons labeled (chosen) as the servants of Yahweh were expected to fulfill special tasks. Abraham was thus expected to go away from his land so that a people would be formed (cf. Gen 12; 17); Moses, the servant of Yahweh, was expected to lead the people from Egypt to the Promised Land; David, the servant of Yahweh, was expected to rule the people of Yahweh (Ps 78.70-71). Even Job, the servant of Yahweh, was not an exception to this: he was expected to show Satan his faithfulness to Yahweh and open a new future for the community. The labeling of Jacob-Israel as the chosen servant of Yahweh (41.8-9) then raised an important question: if the exilic Israel had become the chosen servant, what was the special task that this servant was expected to carry out as the servant of Yahweh?

Second Isaiah answered this question in a two-fold way: (a) he sketched out this servant figure after the model of Moses, who was the servant of Yahweh in order to liberate Israel from the slavery in Egypt and to guide them from that foreign land to the Promised Land (48.20-22; 49.3-4; 50.10; cf. also the coming discussion on Is 50.4-9); the new servant was also expected to carry out a similar mission (cf. 49.5); (b) in the present servant passage (the so-called first servant song, 42.1-4) he clearly outlined the purpose of the present election. According to this text, the servant was expected to bring the teaching (i.e., *tôrāh* which is parallel to *mišpāt*) of Yahweh to the ends of the earth: "(Behold my servant…)

he will not fail or be discouraged till he has established *mišpāt* on the earth; and the coastlands will wait for his teaching" (v 4).

In this short text, the prophet repeats the term *mišpāt* three times and presents it as a synonym of the teaching (*tôrāh*) of Yahweh (v 4); the servant is labelled as the messenger of Yahweh's *mišpāt*; therefore, the interpretation of this noun (which comes from the root *špt*, שפט) seems to be important for the understanding of the concept of the servant.

In Babylon, the title *Šāpitum* (substantive of the root *špt*) was applied to persons with special tasks: a *Šāpitu* had judicial and military authority delegated to him by the ruler (*Šarrum*). He assisted the emperor in the administration of the territory and conducted military campaigns for him.[115]

Notably, similar to the Babylonian *Šāpitum*, the premonarchic judges (*šôpēt*, participle of *špt*) were the vicegerents of Yahweh; they were chosen by Yahweh in order to fulfil special tasks; they were also given the assistance of the spirit of Yahweh (Judg 2.16; 3.9). The noun *mišpāt* can therefore be translated as the rule (of Yahweh).[116] If

---

[115] Cf. The god Šamaš was also called Šāpitu (שפט) which meant that he was the king and judge of both heaven and earth; cf. *CAD*, vol 17, s.v., *Šāpitu*; T. L., Mafico, "Judge, Judging," *ABD* III, 1104-1106.

[116] Several scholars translate the *mišpāt* in this text as 'justice' which is correct in the sense that the servant is expected to bring the justice, i.e., the rule of Yahweh to the ends of the earth. Rule and law are related concepts. Notably, the Babylonian kings/rulers were traditionally law-givers, and legal cases used to be brought to the king; these kings had distinct legal obligations to the cities that

this is so, the servant is expected to bring the rule of Yahweh to the ends of the earth. Thus according to Second Isaiah, the exilic Israel is chosen by the universal emperor Yahweh as his delegate to the ends of the earth (42.1-4). In fact, the prophet sees Yahweh as the mighty emperor who rules the nations from Zion (51.5).

Interestingly, the last verse (v 4) presents *mišpāt* and the teaching (*tôrāh*) of Yahweh as parallel. This is not an isolated text; Is 51.4-5 also does the same: "Listen to me, my people, and give ear to me, my nation; for a teaching (*tôrāh*) will go forth from me, and my rule (*mišpāt*) for a light to the peoples... and my arms will rule (*yišpōtû*, יִשְׁפֹּטוּ) the peoples…"; thus we can say that for Second Isaiah rule of Yahweh and his *tôrāh* are synonyms. Here emerges the following question: what is the meaning of the rule of Yahweh that is a synonym of the teaching of Yahweh in Second Isaiah?

In fact, even when Second Isaiah labels Israel as the servant/vassal of the universal and mighty emperor (Yahweh), he does not visualize a political dominion of Israel above all the nations; he visualizes only the political dominion of Cyrus (the messiah of Yahweh) to whom Yahweh gives power over the kings and authority over their treasures (41.1-4; 45.1-7). The rule of Yahweh of which Israel is the messenger therefore is different from the political conception of an imperial rule.

---

they ruled; Nebuchadnezzar was called the 'king of justice'; J. N. Postgate, "Royal Exercise of Justice under the Assyrian Empire," in *Le palais et la royauté*, 420-421; W. G. Lambert, "Nebuchadnezzar King of Justice," *Iraq* 27 (1965), 1-11.

Notably, all the important persons that were labelled as the servants of Yahweh in the tradition had opened a new future to the people of Yahweh: the election of Abraham marked the formation of a new people; the call of Moses, the servant of Yahweh, marked the beginning of the possession of the Promised Land and the life as a free nation; the covenant with David, the servant of Yahweh, marked the most important stage in the monarchic Israel; the faithfulness of Job pointed to a future different from the past theological notions.

Similarly, here the call of Israel to be the servant of Yahweh unveils a new future for the community. Israel is now chosen as the mandate of Yahweh to bring his teaching to the ends of the earth; it is this teaching that actualises Yahweh's universal rule. The discussion is no more about a political empire; rather, Second Isaiah here visualizes a spiritual empire; it is an empire in which Yahweh's *tôrāh* rules. This rule/teaching will be a light to the peoples: "for a *tôrāh* will go forth from me and my rule for a light to the peoples" (51.4).

What is precisely this teaching of Yahweh that the servant brings to the nations and that is able to realize a universal rule of Yahweh? In several texts Second Isaiah makes it clear that it is monotheism. For example, in 43.10 he declares the purpose of the present election of Israel as the servant of Yahweh: "'You are my *witnesses*,' word of Yahweh, 'and *my servant* whom I have chosen, that *you may know* and *believe me* and *understand* that I am He. Before me no god was formed, nor shall there be any after me'"; in 49.6 it is stated that the servant is appointed as a light to the nations so that salvation may reach to the ends of the earth; in 45.21-22 the prophet categorically declares that salvation for all the nations can only come from Yahweh who is the only God. Similar to the servants of Yahweh who had their tasks to fulfil, now the exilic Israel is chosen as the servant in order to bring the redemptive message of monotheism to the ends of the earth; his mission surpasses the boundaries of space and time.

In fact, 'who is the addressee of this text that begins with a *hēn* (הֵן, behold; 42.1-4)?' is not explicitly stated: it is not the nations (or their gods) or isles because they are referred to in the third person as those who wait for the teaching/rule of Yahweh (42.4); it is not the 'true servant-Israel' because he is the object of the discourse ("I have put my Spirit upon him," v 1). The remaining possibility is that here Yahweh is presenting before the exiles a reinterpreted chosen-servant-ideal ("Behold - הֵן - my servant, whom I will uphold, my chosen"); thus he specifies the special task that those who want to accept this servanthood are expected to realize. Notably, the interjection הֵן is usually used to call the attention of the hearer to some fact upon which action should be taken (Gen 3.22; 4.14; 11.6; 15.3; 19.34; 27.11).

The election to be the servant of Yahweh is thus a call yet to be realized on the part of Israel: the servant is expected to bring (*x-yiqtol*, future) the rule of Yahweh to the nations (v 1). Actually, when the great leaders of Israel were chosen by Yahweh as servants, they were also given the assistance of the spirit of Yahweh in order to fulfill their tasks (cf. Moses and Joshua, Deut 34.9; David, 1Sam 16.13; 2Sam 23.2; Saul, 1Sam 10.6, 10 + 16.14; Elijah, 1King 18.12; Micah, 1King 22.24-25); similarly, this new servant is given the spirit of Yahweh

(42.1). He has to realize his task, that is not limited by geographical boundaries, humbly and silently (v 2-3). He should not faint (*x-yiqtol*, future) until he has brought Yahweh's rule (*mišpāt*) on earth; the isles are waiting for his teaching.

The new servant is thus expected to teach the nations the *tôrāh* of Yahweh. This is the one whom Yahweh will support (אֶתְמָךְ־בּוֹ) and in whom he will take delight (42.1-4). After presenting this servant-ideal, Yahweh reiterates the purpose of this new vocation of Israel in the following verses: "I am Yahweh, I have called you in *ṣedeq* (= redemption) in order to take you by the hand to guard you and to give as a commandment (*b*ᵉ*rîth*)[117] to the people a light to the nations" (42.6). Servanthood is thus a new status of Israel; it is also a goal to be achieved by realizing the appointed task.

6) 42.13-17

13 יְהוָה כַּגִּבּוֹר יֵצֵא כְּאִישׁ מִלְחָמוֹת יָעִיר קִנְאָה
יָרִיעַ אַף־יַצְרִיחַ עַל־אֹיְבָיו יִתְגַּבָּר
14 הֶחֱשֵׁיתִי מֵעוֹלָם אַחֲרִישׁ אֶתְאַפָּק
כַּיּוֹלֵדָה אֶפְעֶה אֶשֹּׁם וְאֶשְׁאַף יָחַד
15 אַחֲרִיב הָרִים וּגְבָעוֹת וְכָל־עֶשְׂבָּם אוֹבִישׁ
וְשַׂמְתִּי נְהָרוֹת לָאִיִּים וַאֲגַמִּים אוֹבִישׁ

---

[117] The first meaning of *b*ᵉ*rîth* (בְּרִית) in Hebrew, Akkadian, and Hittite is not 'agreement between two parties'; it rather implies the notion of 'imposition' or obligation; therefore, a *b*ᵉ*rîth* is commanded (Ps 111.9; Judg 2.20), and it is a synonym of the words law or commandment (Deut 4.13; 33.9; Is 24.5; Ps 50.16; 103.18); cf. M. Weinfeld, "*b*ᵉ*rîth*," *TDOT* II, 253-279.

16 וְהוֹלַכְתִּי עִוְרִים בְּדֶרֶךְ לֹא יָדָעוּ
בִּנְתִיבוֹת לֹא־יָדְעוּ אַדְרִיכֵם
אָשִׂים מַחְשָׁךְ לִפְנֵיהֶם לָאוֹר וּמַעֲקַשִּׁים לְמִישׁוֹר
אֵלֶּה הַדְּבָרִים עֲשִׂיתִם וְלֹא עֲזַבְתִּים
17 נָסֹגוּ אָחוֹר יֵבֹשׁוּ בֹשֶׁת הַבֹּטְחִים בַּפָּסֶל
הָאֹמְרִים לְמַסֵּכָה אַתֶּם אֱלֹהֵינוּ

13 Yahweh will go forth like *a mighty man, like a man of war* he will stir up his fury;

he will cry out, he will shout aloud, *he will show himself mighty against his foes*.

14 For a long time I have held my peace, I would keep still and restrain myself;

now I will *cry out like a woman in travail*, I will gasp and pant.

15 I will *lay waste mountains and hills*, and dry up all their vegetation;

I will turn the rivers into islands, and dry up the pools.

16 And *I will lead the blind in a way that they have not known*;

In paths that they have not known I will guide them.

I will turn the darkness before them into light, the rough places into level ground.

These are the things I have been doing, and I did not forsake them.

17 They shall be turned back and utterly put to shame, who trust in a graven image,

who say to molten images, "You are our gods."

Yahweh, who has apparently lost before the gods, now says that he has not rejected Israel but has called them to be his servant to bring his rule/teaching to the ends of the earth (42.1-4). This appears to the exiles only as an imagination of the prophet. It thus demands an explanation of what is the meaning of the exilic suffering and if Yahweh has not failed before the gods, what has he been doing in this time. These points are clarified in these verses.

Yahweh has not abandoned his people (v 16); he has not failed before the Babylonian gods either; he has only been keeping silence because of the blindness of his people (42.16, 18-19). Now, by contrast, he is coming like a mighty warrior (through Cyrus); he is going to guide the blind people through the ways that they have not known in such a way that the idol-worshippers will be put to shame. Also in this text Yahweh is depicted as a great warrior-emperor (v 13).

Notably here first Yahweh is depicted as a fierce warrior (v 13); then he is depicted as a woman (who cries) in travail (v 14); then he is depicted as one who destroys mountains and dries pools (v 15); then he is depicted as the one who guides Israel in a second exodus (v 16); at last it is announced that the idol-makers will be put to shame. In fact, here there is an apparent juxtaposition of metaphors.

This accumulation of metaphors gives rise at least to three questions: 1) what is the relationship between the shouting and destroying warrior (vv 13, 15) and a woman in travail who cries to give birth to something (v 14)? 2) What is the relationship between a woman in travail and an exodus guided by Yahweh (v 16)? 3) What is the relationship between these images and the final declaration of the shame of the idol-worshippers (v 17)?

In fact, these are very closely related metaphors in Second Isaiah. The prophet depicts Yahweh as the universal emperor in order to show his superiority over the nations (cf. Is 40.12-31). Now Yahweh comes like a warrior and acts through Cyrus in order to redeem his people from Babylon because he has not rejected them (cf. 48.14-15); for Israel, this redemption is a call to return to the city of Yahweh which implies a new exodus (44.21-22; 48.20-21; 52.11-12). This exodus will be the occasion in which Israel will be regenerated; therefore, he brings the metaphor of panting the woman. Yahweh will recreate them as his servant (cf. 44.1-5); this is a second exodus which is similar to the first one because according to the tradition, it was during the exodus from Egypt that Israel was first formed to be the people of Yahweh (cf. Ex 19); now the prophet is calling for a second exodus through which Israel will be regenerated to be the servant/mandate of the only God.

This regeneration will result in the shame of the idol-worshippers because this is a regeneration that helps them to announce pro-Yahweh monotheism (43.21); this is the teaching/rule of Yahweh. These points find clearer expositions in the coming poems; therefore, they will be discussed in the following pages through the analysis of the texts.

7) 42.18-25

18 הַחֵרְשִׁים שְׁמָעוּ וְהַעִוְרִים הַבִּיטוּ לִרְאוֹת
19 מִי עִוֵּר כִּי אִם־עַבְדִּי וְחֵרֵשׁ כְּמַלְאָכִי אֶשְׁלָח
מִי עִוֵּר כִּמְשֻׁלָּם וְעִוֵּר כְּעֶבֶד יְהוָה
20 רָאִיתָ רַבּוֹת וְלֹא תִשְׁמֹר פָּקוֹחַ אָזְנַיִם וְלֹא יִשְׁמָע

21 יְהוָה חָפֵץ לְמַעַן צִדְקוֹ יַגְדִּיל תּוֹרָה וְיַאְדִּיר
22 וְהוּא עַם־בָּזוּז וְשָׁסוּי הָפֵחַ בַּחוּרִים כֻּלָּם וּבְבָתֵּי כְלָאִים הָחְבָּאוּ
הָיוּ לָבַז וְאֵין מַצִּיל מְשִׁסָּה וְאֵין־אֹמֵר הָשַׁב
23 מִי בָכֶם יַאֲזִין זֹאת יַקְשִׁב וְיִשְׁמַע לְאָחוֹר
24 מִי־נָתַן לִמְשִׁסָּה יַעֲקֹב וְיִשְׂרָאֵל לְבֹזְזִים
הֲלוֹא יְהוָה זוּ חָטָאנוּ לוֹ
וְלֹא־אָבוּ בִדְרָכָיו הָלוֹךְ וְלֹא שָׁמְעוּ בְּתוֹרָתוֹ
25 וַיִּשְׁפֹּךְ עָלָיו חֵמָה אַפּוֹ וֶעֱזוּז מִלְחָמָה
וַתְּלַהֲטֵהוּ מִסָּבִיב וְלֹא יָדָע וַתִּבְעַר־בּוֹ וְלֹא־יָשִׂים עַל־לֵב

18 Hear, you deaf, and look, you blind, that you may see!

19 Who is blind but *my servant*, and deaf as my messenger whom I will send?

Who is blind like the one committed to me, and blind as the *servant of Yahweh*?

20 *He has seen many things, but did not observe* them; his ears are open, but he did not hear.

21 Yahweh is well pleased for his redemptions' sake; he will magnify his *teaching* and *make it glorious*.

22 But this is a people robbed and plundered, all of them trapped in holes and hidden in prisons;

They have become a prey with none to rescue, a spoil with none to say, "Restore!"

23 Who among you will listen to this, will attend to hear about the time to come?

24 *Who gave up Jacob for plunder and Israel to the robbers?*

Was it not Yahweh, against whom we have sinned, in whose ways they did not walk, and whose teaching they did not obey?

25 He poured upon him the heat of his anger and the *might of battle*;

> It set him on fire round about, but he did not understand; it burned him, but he did not take it to heart.

This is a text in which the noun servant (*'ebed*) appears twice. The exilic Israel is once again undoubtedly labeled as the servant and messenger (מַלְאָךְ) of Yahweh: "Who is blind but my servant, or deaf as my messenger whom I will send? Who is blind … as the servant of Yahweh … Yahweh was pleased… to magnify his *teaching*… Who gave up Jacob to the spoiler and Israel to the robbers? Was it not Yahweh ... whose *tôrāh* they would not obey?" (vv 19-24).

The text confirms the idea that the noun *'ebed* (in the singular) designates a corporate reality: in v 19 it is used in singular with corresponding adjectives (עִוֵּר, חֵרֵשׁ); by contrast, in v 24 the verbs are in the plural (חָטָאנוּ, אָבוּ, שָׁמְעוּ), and the servant is addressed as Jacob and Israel. In v 25 again the verbal forms and the pronouns appear in singular. According to this text, thus, the noun servant in singular designates Israel which is a plural entity. This text also underlines the exilic life-setting of the servant (v 22).

Even though chosen to fulfill a great task (41.8-9; 42.1-4), the servant is blind and deaf (42.16, 19). These blindness and deafness are metaphorical because he in fact sees and hears much although he does not grasp anything (vv 19-20). Yahweh wants to magnify his teaching and bring his rule to the ends of the earth. His servant/people, however, did not obey his teaching in such a way to walk in his ways; as a result, Yahweh sent them (Jacob-Israel) away (v 24). The duty of a servant (vassal) is to obey his master, but this servant rebelled.

Yahweh, the warrior, then poured upon them the might of his battle; here Yahweh is fighting against his own people. The incomprehension of Israel is tremendous in such a degree that even when the fury of Yahweh burned them all around, they did not know (וְלֹא יָדָע) and did not understand (וְלֹא יָשִׂים עַל לֵב, v 25).

Clearly, this figure of the servant does not correspond to the servant-ideal already outlined by Yahweh, i.e., an obedient and spirit-filled servant who brings / teaches Yahweh's *tôrāh* (rule) to the ends of the earth (42.1-4). Yahweh, the great warrior, will therefore destroy the mountains; he will make this blind servant walk through the ways that he has not known, and change the darkness on his way into light in order to make the blind see (cf. 42.16): according to the Yahweh-alone party, walking in the ways of Yahweh meant obedience to Yahweh's commandments, while walking away from Yahweh signified disobedience.[118]

---

118 Prophet Hosea accused Israel of idolatry by saying: "The more I called them, the more they *went away from me* (הלך) to the Baals, and kept sacrificing and burning incense to idols" (11.2). Deuteronomy exhorted Israel to walk in the ways of Yahweh: "You shall *walk in all the way* which Yahweh your God has commanded you, that you may live … and that you may prolong your days in the land which you shall possess" (5.33). Jeremiah blamed people for rejecting Yahweh which according to him was a walking backward; this false walking caused the destruction of Israel: "You have rejected me, says Yahweh, you *kept going backward*; so I have stretched out my hand upon you and destroyed you; I am weary of relenting" (15.6); walking away from Yahweh meant worship of other gods as well (Deut 13.4-6). At the same time walking in the ways of Yahweh will lead to salvation: "For I command you today to love Yahweh your God to *walk in his ways*

In this text the prophet democratizes the religious responsibility ("Who gave up Jacob to the spoiler? ... Was it not Yahweh, against whom *we have sinned*" v 24); he also calls the exiles to give heed to his message that unveils the divine plan for their future (v 23). Yahweh will now cry out and shout aloud like a warrior and like a woman in labor in order to make this deaf servant hear (v 13, 14); Yahweh is acting like a warrior (to redeem from Babylon) and a panting woman in order to give birth to a new reality. As mentioned above, these divine actions will result in the shame of the idol-worshippers: "They shall be greatly ashamed, those trust in graven images that say to the molten images, 'You are our gods'" (v 17). The relationship between the servanthood / regeneration of Israel and the shame of the idol-worshippers will be discussed in the next servant passage (43.10-13).

8) 43.1-7

1 וְעַתָּה כֹּה־אָמַר יְהוָה בֹּרַאֲךָ יַעֲקֹב וְיֹצֶרְךָ יִשְׂרָאֵל
אַל־תִּירָא כִּי גְאַלְתִּיךָ קָרָאתִי בְשִׁמְךָ לִי־אָתָּה
2 כִּי־תַעֲבֹר בַּמַּיִם אִתְּךָ־אָנִי וּבַנְּהָרוֹת לֹא יִשְׁטְפוּךָ
כִּי־תֵלֵךְ בְּמוֹ־אֵשׁ לֹא תִכָּוֶה וְלֶהָבָה לֹא תִבְעַר־בָּךְ
3 כִּי אֲנִי יְהוָה אֱלֹהֶיךָ קְדוֹשׁ יִשְׂרָאֵל מוֹשִׁיעֶךָ

(הלך), and to keep his commandments and his statutes and his ordinances, then you shall live and multiply, and Yahweh your God will bless you in the land …" (Deut 30.16; also 5.33; 8.6; 19.9; 26.17; 28.9). It also means to worship Yahweh: "And now, Israel, what does Yahweh your God require of you, if not to fear Yahweh, your God, to *walk in all his ways*, to love him, to worship (עבר) Yahweh your God with all your heart and with all your soul" (Deut 10.12); cf. also Jer 7.22-23.

נָתַתִּי כָפְרְךָ מִצְרַיִם כּוּשׁ וּסְבָא תַּחְתֶּיךָ
מֵאֲשֶׁר יָקַרְתָּ בְעֵינַי נִכְבַּדְתָּ וַאֲנִי אֲהַבְתִּיךָ 4
וְאֶתֵּן אָדָם תַּחְתֶּיךָ וּלְאֻמִּים תַּחַת נַפְשֶׁךָ
אַל־תִּירָא כִּי אִתְּךָ־אָנִי 5
מִמִּזְרָח אָבִיא זַרְעֶךָ וּמִמַּעֲרָב אֲקַבְּצֶךָּ
אֹמַר לַצָּפוֹן תֵּנִי וּלְתֵימָן אַל־תִּכְלָאִי 6
הָבִיאִי בָנַי מֵרָחוֹק וּבְנוֹתַי מִקְצֵה הָאָרֶץ
כֹּל הַנִּקְרָא בִשְׁמִי וְלִכְבוֹדִי בְּרָאתִיו יְצַרְתִּיו אַף־עֲשִׂיתִיו 7

[1] But now thus said Yahweh, he who creates you, O Jacob, he who forms you, O Israel:

"Fear not, for I have redeemed you; I have called you by name, you are mine.

[2] When you will pass through the waters I am with you; and through the rivers, they shall not overwhelm you;

when you will walk through fire you shall not be burned, and the flame shall not consume you.

[3] For I am Yahweh your God, the Holy One of Israel is your Savior.

I have given Egypt as your ransom, Ethiopia and Seba in exchange for you,

[4] because you are precious in my eyes, and honored, and I love you,

That I may give (*weyiqtol*) men in return for you, peoples in exchange for your life.

[5] Fear not, for I am with you;

I will bring your offspring from the east, and from the west I will gather you;

[6] *I will say to the north, Give up, and to the south, Do not withhold;*

(you) Bring my sons from afar and my daughters from the

end of the earth,

7 every one who is called by my name, whom I created for my glory, whom I formed and made."

In this text, which is delimited by the theme of the creation of Israel (Yahweh, he who creates you... who forms you), Yahweh again appears as the great emperor who regenerates Israel (v 7, also v 1); he is going to act with power; with great authority, he will command to the north and south to liberate his sons and daughters. By calling Israel the sons and daughters of Yahweh, Israel is implicitly presented as the vassal and mandate of Yahweh.

We already mentioned that in the ancient Near Eastern treaties between the emperor and the vassal, the lord-servant language, which was interchangeable with father-son, was employed: the vassals were also called the sons of the emperors (cf. 2King 16.7-9). In addition, these great emperors and kings were also called the sons of their gods or goddess.[119] For example, Šulgi was carried in the sacred womb of the goddess Ninsuna; King Gudea says to goddess Gatumdug: "You took my fathers seed into your womb; you bore me in the sanctuary," meaning that he was formed in the womb of his mother;[120] Simi-

[119] Jacobsen, *The Treasures*, 158-159.

[120] For a number of other cases cf. S. N. Kramer, "Kingship in Sumer and Akkad: The Ideal King," in *Le palais et la royauté*, ed. P. Garelli, Paris, Librairie orientaliste Paul Geuthner, 1974, 167; R. Labat, *Le caractère religieux de la royauté assyro-babylonienne* (EA 1), Paris, Libraire d'Amérique et d'Orient, 1939, 58; Frankfort, *Kingship*, 238, 299-301.

larly, Nabonidus was said to be called by Sîn to kingship from the womb of his mother (building inscription 15, col 1, 4-5).[121]

Alluding to these ancient Near Eastern political conceptions, Second Isaiah presented Jacob-Israel as the royal servant of Yahweh, whom Yahweh formed in the womb: "Now thus said Yahweh, he who creates you, O Jacob, he who forms you, O Israel" (43.1); "Thus said Yahweh who makes you, who forms you from the womb" (44.2); "Hearken to me, O house of Jacob, and all the remnant of the house of Israel, who have been borne (by me) from the womb, who have been carried (by me) from the uterus" (46.3; see also 44.24; 49.1, 5). This text thus clarifies why the prophet employed the metaphor of the panting woman in the previous text (42.14).

At the same time, this was a reinterpretation of the traditional royal servant of Yahweh concept. According to the tradition, Davidic king was the son of Yahweh. For example, in the second psalm we read the following proclamation of David: "He (Yahweh) said to me, 'you are my son, today I have begotten you'" (Ps 2.7); in the message of Yahweh to David through Nathan the following promise was made: "Now therefore thus you (Nathan) shall say to *my servant* David, 'Thus said Yahweh ... when your days are fulfilled and you lie down with your fathers, I will raise up your offspring after you, who shall come forth from your body ... I will establish the throne of his kingdom for ever. I will be his *father*,

---

[121] Also in Egypt, the Pharaoh was thought to be born of Amun; cf. H. Ringgren, "*melek*," *TDOT* VIII, 349-350.

and he shall be *my son*'" (2Sam 7.8-14; see also 1Chr 17.13; 22.10; 28.6).

Psalm 89 celebrated a covenant between Yahweh and his earthly mandate/servant David (vv 3, 20) that proclaimed the king as the son of Yahweh: "He (David) shall cry to me, 'you are my father, my God, and the rock of my salvation'; and I will make him the first-born, the highest of the kings of the earth'" (vv 27-28). In the Isaianic reinterpretation of the servant concept, the exilic Israel became the son of Yahweh who was loved by his God: "(Israel) you are precious in my eyes, and honored, and I love you" (Is 43.4); this seems to be an answer to the exilic crisis implied in the questions like the following: "Lord, where is your steadfast love (חֶסֶד) of old, which in your faithfulness you swore to David?" (Ps 89.49).

In fact, this text explicates two concepts about the exilic notion of the servant of Yahweh: a) the servant is expected to walk through fire and waters but Yahweh will be with him (v 2). This is comparable to the life experience of Job, the servant of Yahweh. b) Yahweh has abandoned Egypt and Seba, and taken Israel (3; compare Deut 14.2). It is the love of Yahweh that prompts him to choose Israel as his servant.

9) 43.10-13

10 אַתֶּם עֵדַי נְאֻם־יְהוָה וְעַבְדִּי אֲשֶׁר בָּחָרְתִּי
לְמַעַן תֵּדְעוּ וְתַאֲמִינוּ לִי וְתָבִינוּ כִּי־אֲנִי הוּא
לְפָנַי לֹא־נוֹצַר אֵל וְאַחֲרַי לֹא יִהְיֶה
11 אָנֹכִי אָנֹכִי יְהוָה וְאֵין מִבַּלְעָדַי מוֹשִׁיעַ
12 אָנֹכִי הִגַּדְתִּי וְהוֹשַׁעְתִּי וְהִשְׁמַעְתִּי וְאֵין בָּכֶם זָר

וְאַתֶּם עֵדַי נְאֻם־יְהוָה וַאֲנִי־אֵל
13 גַּם־מִיּוֹם אֲנִי הוּא וְאֵין מִיָּדִי מַצִּיל אֶפְעַל וּמִי יְשִׁיבֶנָּה

[10] "You are my *witnesses*," word of Yahweh, "and *my servant* whom I have chosen,

So that *you may know* and believe me and understand that I am He.

Before me no god was formed, nor will there be any after me.

[11] I, I am Yahweh, and besides me there is no savior.

[12] I declared and saved and proclaimed, and there was no stranger (god) among you;

And you are my witnesses," word of Yahweh.

[13] "I am God, and also henceforth I am He; there is no one who can deliver from my hand; I work and who will reverse it?"

This text which labels Israel as the servant answers the previously raised question on the relationship between the servanthood of Israel and the shame of the idol-worshippers (42.17). Yahweh explicitly tells Israel that he has chosen them (בחר) as his servant and witness so that they should understand that he is the only God. In order to fulfill this task as the witness of Yahweh, first this servant himself *has to know* (ידע), *believe* (אמן) and *understand* (בין) Yahweh as the only God (vv 10-12) and that besides him there is no other divinity and redeemer (v 13).

This text thus specifies that the servanthood and the consequent task of Israel (cf. 42.1-4) are linked with pro-Yahweh monotheism; Israel has yet to understand Yahweh as the only God. If they understand this and then carry this teaching (*tôrāh*) to the ends of the earth (42.1, 4), the idol-worshippers, who speak to their idols "you are our gods" will be put to shame (42.17). The right comprehension of Israel about Yahweh is the way to establish the universal rule of Yahweh.

Unfortunately, Israel is still blind and deaf to this reality (42.16-19; 43.8). The abovementioned blindness and deafness of Israel thus consists in the lack of understanding (cf. 42.16, 18-19, 25). In exile, Yahweh announces them that he will lead them through the ways that they have not known (42.16): in exile, devoid of any other redeemer (v 22), Israel will know that it is Yahweh who sent them into exile because they disobeyed his teaching (42.24). In fact, the Yahweh-alone party used to accuse the pre-exilic Israel of the lack of knowledge of Yahweh (Deut 32.28-29; Jer 10.14; 51.17; Hos 4.6). Second Isaiah is taking this lack of knowledge of Israel about their God as an important point of discussion.

10) 43.16-21

16 כֹּה אָמַר יְהוָה הַנּוֹתֵן בַּיָּם דָּרֶךְ וּבְמַיִם עַזִּים נְתִיבָה
17 הַמּוֹצִיא רֶכֶב־וָסוּס חַיִל וְעִזּוּז יַחְדָּו
יִשְׁכְּבוּ בַּל־יָקוּמוּ דָּעֲכוּ כַּפִּשְׁתָּה כָבוּ
18 אַל־תִּזְכְּרוּ רִאשֹׁנוֹת וְקַדְמֹנִיּוֹת אַל־תִּתְבֹּנָנוּ
19 הִנְנִי עֹשֶׂה חֲדָשָׁה עַתָּה תִצְמָח הֲלוֹא תֵדָעוּהָ
אַף אָשִׂים בַּמִּדְבָּר דֶּרֶךְ בִּישִׁמוֹן נְהָרוֹת
20 תְּכַבְּדֵנִי חַיַּת הַשָּׂדֶה תַּנִּים וּבְנוֹת יַעֲנָה
כִּי־נָתַתִּי בַמִּדְבָּר מַיִם נְהָרוֹת בִּישִׁימֹן לְהַשְׁקוֹת עַמִּי בְחִירִי
21 עַם־זוּ יָצַרְתִּי לִי תְּהִלָּתִי יְסַפֵּרוּ

[16] Thus said Yahweh, *who makes a way in the sea, a path in the mighty waters,*
[17] *who brings forth chariot and horse, army and warrior together*;
They will lie down, they will not rise, they *are extinguished*, quenched like a wick:
[18] "Remember not the former things, nor consider the things of old.
[19] Behold, *I am doing a new thing*; now it will spring forth, *do you not perceive it*?
I will make *a way in the wilderness* and rivers in the desert.
[20] The wild beasts will honor me, the jackals and the ostriches;
For I have given water in the wilderness, rivers in the desert, to give drink to my chosen people,
[21] *The people whom I will have formed for myself will declare my praise.*

According to this text, Yahweh is an extraordinary warrior who even makes a way in the waters, who brings forth chariots and horses in such a way that the enemies will be extinguished and quenched like a wick. The prophet is here making an allusion to their exodus journey from Egypt in which Israel was first formed to be the people of Yahweh.[122] This Yahweh now says to Israel

---

[122] In verses 16-17, familiar phrases from the exodus tradition are employed in order to recall the historical redemptive actions of Yahweh: a way through the mighty waters (Ex 15.19), and horses and drivers drowned (Ex 15.1, 4, 10, 19, 21; Deut 11.4; also Ex 14.9, 23).

that they will forget the former things[123] because he is going to create a new thing.

The following verses spell out what the newly created thing is: Yahweh will make a way in the desert (a new exodus, v 19); through this exodus he will recreate Israel (v 18); consequently, the newly created people will announce Yahweh's glory (v 21). The process of regeneration is already visible: "Behold, I am doing a new thing; now it will spring forth, do you not perceive it?" (v 19). The already visible process of regeneration may either be an allusion to the already perceptible arrival of Cyrus for the redemption of Israel that will mark the beginning of a new exodus, or an allusion to the work of the Yahweh-alone party that already announces monotheism.

This text -- that links the military figure of Yahweh to the new creation of Israel, a new exodus, and the consequent glorification of Yahweh -- makes it clear that the Isaianic appeal to the exodus tradition of Israel

---

[123] There are two similar passages in Jeremiah (also a Yahweh-alonist) that speak about the glory of the new exodus: "Therefore, behold, the days are coming, says Yahweh, when it shall no longer be said, 'as Yahweh lives who brought up the sons of Israel out of the land of Egypt,' but 'as Yahweh lives who brought up the people of Israel out of the north country and out of all the countries where he had driven them,' for I will bring them back to their own land which I gave to their fathers" (16.14-15; also 23.7-8). It can therefore be concluded that in this text 'the former things' (Is 43.18) primarily refer to the redemptive actions of Yahweh in the exodus from Egypt. In that exodus, Yahweh redeemed his people without any help from a foreigner and gave them water in the desert (v 20); for the present exodus, however, a foreigner, Cyrus, will be brought to work out the salvation.

intends to communicate the notion of their regeneration in the desert.

11) 44.1-5

וְעַתָּה שְׁמַע יַעֲקֹב עַבְדִּי וְיִשְׂרָאֵל בָּחַרְתִּי בוֹ 1
כֹּה־אָמַר יְהוָה עֹשֶׂךָ וְיֹצֶרְךָ מִבֶּטֶן יַעְזְרֶךָּ 2
אַל־תִּירָא עַבְדִּי יַעֲקֹב וִישֻׁרוּן בָּחַרְתִּי בוֹ 3
כִּי אֶצָּק־מַיִם עַל־צָמֵא וְנֹזְלִים עַל־יַבָּשָׁה
אֶצֹּק רוּחִי עַל־זַרְעֶךָ וּבִרְכָתִי עַל־צֶאֱצָאֶיךָ
וְצָמְחוּ בְּבֵין חָצִיר כַּעֲרָבִים עַל־יִבְלֵי־מָיִם 4
זֶה יֹאמַר לַיהוָה אָנִי וְזֶה יִקְרָא בְשֵׁם־יַעֲקֹב 5
וְזֶה יִכְתֹּב יָדוֹ לַיהוָה וּבְשֵׁם יִשְׂרָאֵל יְכַנֶּה

[1] "But now hear, O Jacob *my servant*, Israel whom I have chosen!

[2] Thus said Yahweh, who makes you, who *forms you from the womb* and will help you:

Fear not, O Jacob *my servant*, *Jeshurun* whom I have chosen.

[3] For *I will pour water on the thirsty*, and flows on the dry ground;

I will pour my *spirit upon your descendants*, and my blessing on your offspring.

[4] They *shall spring up* like grass amid waters, like willows by flowing streams.

[5] This one will say, 'I am Yahweh's,' another will call himself by the name of Jacob,

And another will write on his hand, 'Yahweh's,' and surname himself by the name of Israel."

The previous text spoke about the regeneration of Israel by the Emperor Yahweh. The present text, that reconfirms Jacob-Israel as Yahweh's chosen servant (בחר, vv 1, 2), specifies how this regeneration will take place and why: "I (Yahweh) will pour water on the thirsty ... I will pour my spirit upon your descendants... they (Israel) shall spring up like grass amid waters, like willows by flowing streams'" (vv 1, 2, 4). In fact, this idea of regeneration is the running theme: in 42.14 it was presented through the metaphor of the panting woman who cries out like a woman in labour; in 42.9 and 43.19 Yahweh announced the creation of a new thing (also 43.1, 7); according to the present text Yahweh forms Israel from the womb (44.1-2); in 45.9-10 Yahweh will harshly rebuke those who do not cooperate with this regeneration.

The chosen servants of Yahweh, according to the tradition, received certain divine promises: Abraham received the promise of the land and a nation; Moses realized this promise (Ex 19.5-6), David received the promise of the kingdom. These servants also received the assistance of the spirit of Yahweh (Deut 34.9; Is 11.1-2). Now Second Isaiah announces that Yahweh is regenerating Israel as his servant; this declaration is accompanied by two promises: regeneration by pouring out of his spirit upon the exiles, and a glorious future as a monotheistic community.

Through this regeneration, Yahweh will realize the already projected servant-ideal (42.1). As the result there will emerge a new Jacob-Israel, a covenant community dedicated to Yahweh: "This one will say, 'I am Yahweh's,' another will call himself by the name of Jacob..." (44.5). As already mentioned, the purpose of the election of Israel as the servant is the formation of a monotheistic community dedicated to Yahweh (43.10-11); once the community is formed, they will be the mandates of the only God: "the people whom I will have formed for myself will declare my praise" (43.21).

12) 44.6-8

6 כֹּה־אָמַר יְהוָה מֶלֶךְ־יִשְׂרָאֵל וְגֹאֲלוֹ יְהוָה צְבָאאת
אֲנִי רִאשׁוֹן וַאֲנִי אַחֲרוֹן וּמִבַּלְעָדַי אֵין אֱלֹהִים
7 וּמִי־כָמוֹנִי יִקְרָא וְיַגִּידֶהָ וְיַעְרְכֶהָ לִי
מִשּׂוּמִי עַם־עוֹלָם וְאֹתִיּוֹת וַאֲשֶׁר תָּבֹאנָה יַגִּידוּ לָמוֹ
8 אַל־תִּפְחֲדוּ וְאַל־תִּרְהוּ הֲלֹא מֵאָז הִשְׁמַעְתִּיךְ וְהִגַּדְתִּי
וְאַתֶּם עֵדָי הֲיֵשׁ אֱלוֹהַּ מִבַּלְעָדַי וְאֵין צוּר בַּל־יָדָעְתִּי

6 Thus said Yahweh, *the King of Israel and his Redeemer, the Lord of Hosts*:

"*I am the first and I am the last; besides me there is no god.*

7 Who is like me? Let him proclaim it, let him declare and set it forth before me.

Who has announced from of old the things to come? Let them tell us what is yet to be.

8 Fear not, nor be afraid; have I not told you from of old and declared it?

And you are my witnesses! *Is there a God besides me?* There is no rock; I know not any."

Reaffirming the already presented divine image, this text presents Yahweh as the only God and king of Israel (cf. also 43.14-15), and as the lord of hosts (יְהוָה צְבָאוֹת); he is their king and redeemer; he is the only God; Israel is his witness. According to the biblical tradition, the title 'lord of hosts' is connected to the idea of Yahweh as *warrior and king*:[124] it appears in connection with the ark-narrative and with the sanctuary in Shiloh (1Sam 4.4; 2Sam 6.2; 1Chr 13.6). Notably, Yahweh was the divine warrior who fought for David (1Sam 17.45).[125] This divine warrior-redeemer of David (the royal servant of Yahweh) has now become the redeemer (divine warrior) of the new servant of Yahweh - Israel.

In the ancient Near East, gods of the nations were often labeled as the rocks in the sense that they gave birth to their people (cf. Deut 32.31, 37). Declaring himself as the only God and redeemer, Yahweh totally rejects this popular notion: "Is there a God besides me? There is no rock." Yahweh does not know about the existence of another rock. According to Deuteronomist (32.18) Yahweh is the rock that regenerates Israel.[126]

13) 44.21-22

21 זְכָר־אֵלֶּה יַעֲקֹב וְיִשְׂרָאֵל כִּי עַבְדִּי־אָתָּה
יְצַרְתִּיךְ עֶבֶד־לִי אַתָּה יִשְׂרָאֵל לֹא תִנָּשֵׁנִי

[124] The title 'lord of hosts' occurs altogether six times in Second Isaiah. *El ṣebaot* was the chief god of the Canaanite pantheon and was the ultimate king in Ugarit.

[125] The title is frequently attested in Isaiah of Jerusalem and in the Zion tradition (Is 6.3-5; 8.18). In the Zion Psalms, Zion is called the city of the great king (48.3). It is connected with the Baal tradition as well; cf. C. L. Seow, "The Lord of Hosts," *ABD* III, 304-307.

[126] See a discussion on this theme in M.S. Smith, "Monotheism in Isaiah 40-55," 191.

22
מָחִיתִי כָעָב פְּשָׁעֶיךָ וְכֶעָנָן חַטֹּאותֶיךָ
שׁוּבָה אֵלַי כִּי גְאַלְתִּיךָ

[21] Remember these things, O Jacob and Israel, for you are *my servant*;

I *formed* you, you are *my servant*; O Israel, you will not be forgotten by me.

[22] I have swept away your transgressions like a cloud, and your sins like mist;

Return to me, for I have redeemed you.

This servant text confirms once again that the prophet is speaking about the regeneration of Jacob-Israel as the servant of Yahweh; Yahweh has not rejected them. As mentioned above, to be the servant of Yahweh, the exilic Israel needs regeneration.

This servant will not be forgotten by Yahweh (לֹא תִנָּשֵׁנִי). This promise assures the exiles of redemption; it is also an affirmation of the faithfulness of Yahweh (cf. Lam 5.20: "Why do you always forget us?"). The text declares how Yahweh regenerates his servant, viz., by wiping out *their* transgressions (not the transgression of the king) and by redeeming them (גאל): it is a formation / regeneration (יצר) that redeems (גאל) by wiping out their iniquities (מחה). According to the Yahweh-alone party, lack of knowledge of Yahweh is the iniquity of the people (Deut 32.28-29; Jer 10.14; 51.17; Hos 4.6). This ignorance swayed them to go away from Yahweh and look to the idols as gods. Now Yahweh is going to regenerate them as monotheists by wiping out their transgressions.

In this process of regeneration Yahweh also needs their cooperation by returning from their idols: "return to me" (44.22). This call to return is preceded by an idol-passage (44.9-20, followed by a "remember these things"). They should learn from Yahweh (48.17-19; 50.4). This text thus confirms the previously stated idea that the servanthood of Israel is linked with pro-Yahweh monotheism (42.17; 43.10-13).

14) 44.24-28

24 כֹּה־אָמַר יְהוָה גֹּאֲלֶךָ וְיֹצֶרְךָ מִבָּטֶן
אָנֹכִי יְהוָה עֹשֶׂה כֹּל
נֹטֶה שָׁמַיִם לְבַדִּי רֹקַע הָאָרֶץ מִי אִתִּי
25 מֵפֵר אֹתוֹת בַּדִּים וְקֹסְמִים יְהוֹלֵל
מֵשִׁיב חֲכָמִים אָחוֹר וְדַעְתָּם יְשַׂכֵּל
26 מֵקִים דְּבַר עַבְדּוֹ וַעֲצַת מַלְאָכָיו יַשְׁלִים
הָאֹמֵר לִירוּשָׁלַםִ תּוּשָׁב וּלְעָרֵי יְהוּדָה תִּבָּנֶינָה וְחָרְבוֹתֶיהָ אֲקוֹמֵם
27 הָאֹמֵר לַצּוּלָה חֳרָבִי וְנַהֲרֹתַיִךְ אוֹבִישׁ
28 הָאֹמֵר לְכוֹרֶשׁ רֹעִי וְכָל־חֶפְצִי יַשְׁלִם
וְלֵאמֹר לִירוּשָׁלַםִ תִּבָּנֶה וְהֵיכָל תִּוָּסֵד

24 Thus said Yahweh, your redeemer, *who forms you from the womb*:
"I am Yahweh, who makes all things,
Who stretches out the heavens alone,
Who spreads out the earth -- Who is with me? –
25 Who frustrates the omens of liars, and will make fools the diviners;
Who turns wise men back, and will make their knowledge foolish;

[26] Who confirms the word of *his servant*, and will fulfill the counsel of *his messengers*;
Who says of Jerusalem, 'She shall be inhabited,' and of the cities of Judah, 'They shall be built, and I will raise up their ruins';
[27] Who says to the deep, 'Be dry, I will dry up your rivers';
[28] *Who says of Cyrus, 'He is my shepherd, and he shall fulfill all my purpose*';
saying of Jerusalem, 'She shall be built,' and of the temple, 'its foundation shall be laid.'"

This text in which the substantive servant (*'ebed*) occurs clarifies further the lord-servant metaphor and elucidates the already made promise of a glorious future. It says that Yahweh alone is the creator of everything and the one who controls history. He creates the heaven and earth; he confirms the words of his messengers; he directs Cyrus. All these affirmations climaxes in the promise that Judah will be restored. Yahweh is the redeemer of Israel and the great emperor who brings Cyrus; he will rebuild Judah. In 44.26 the servant is seen as the *messenger of Yahweh* (cf. 42.19; cf. 42.1-4), whose words will be confirmed by the God of Israel. Yahweh is the one who forms his servant in the womb. The regeneration of the servant and the restoration of the Promised Land mean the same thing, because regeneration also implies their return to the ancestral land.

15) 45.1-7

1 כֹּה־אָמַר יְהוָה לִמְשִׁיחוֹ לְכוֹרֶשׁ אֲשֶׁר־הֶחֱזַקְתִּי בִימִינוֹ
לְרַד־לְפָנָיו גּוֹיִם וּמָתְנֵי מְלָכִים אֲפַתֵּחַ

לִפְתֹּחַ לְפָנָיו דְּלָתַיִם וּשְׁעָרִים לֹא יִסָּגֵרוּ
2 אֲנִי לְפָנֶיךָ אֵלֵךְ וַהֲדוּרִים אֲיַשֵּׁר
דַּלְתוֹת נְחוּשָׁה אֲשַׁבֵּר וּבְרִיחֵי בַרְזֶל אֲגַדֵּעַ
3 וְנָתַתִּי לְךָ אוֹצְרוֹת חֹשֶׁךְ וּמַטְמֻנֵי מִסְתָּרִים
לְמַעַן תֵּדַע כִּי־אֲנִי יְהוָה הַקּוֹרֵא בְשִׁמְךָ אֱלֹהֵי יִשְׂרָאֵל
4 לְמַעַן עַבְדִּי יַעֲקֹב וְיִשְׂרָאֵל בְּחִירִי
וָאֶקְרָא לְךָ בִּשְׁמֶךָ אֲכַנְּךָ וְלֹא יְדַעְתָּנִי
5 אֲנִי יְהוָה וְאֵין עוֹד זוּלָתִי אֵין אֱלֹהִים
אֲאַזֶּרְךָ וְלֹא יְדַעְתָּנִי
6 לְמַעַן יֵדְעוּ מִמִּזְרַח־שֶׁמֶשׁ וּמִמַּעֲרָבָה כִּי־אֶפֶס בִּלְעָדָי
אֲנִי יְהוָה וְאֵין עוֹד
7 יוֹצֵר אוֹר וּבוֹרֵא חֹשֶׁךְ עֹשֶׂה שָׁלוֹם וּבוֹרֵא רָע
אֲנִי יְהוָה עֹשֶׂה כָל־אֵלֶּה

1 Thus said Yahweh to his anointed, to Cyrus, *whose right hand I have grasped,*

to subdue nations before him and the loins of kings I will open,

To open doors before him that gates will not be shut:

2 "I will go before you and level the mountains,

I will break in pieces the doors of bronze and cut asunder the bars of iron,

3 I will give you the treasures of darkness and riches hidden in secret places,

That you may know that I am Yahweh, the God of Israel, who calls you by your name.

4 For the sake of *my servant Jacob*, and Israel my chosen,

I have called you by your name; I will surname you, though you did not know me.

5 I am Yahweh, and there is no other, besides me there is no God;

I will gird you, though you did not know me,
[6] That *men may know, from the rising of the sun and from the west, that there is none besides me*;
I am Yahweh, and there is no other.
[7] I form light and create darkness, I make weal and create woe, I am Yahweh who do all these things.

The previous text labeled the victorious Cyrus as the shepherd of Yahweh and announced that the city of Yahweh will be rebuilt; the present text calls Cyrus as the messiah of Yahweh. Yahweh is the greatest authority who even directs the most victorious earthly emperor and gives him victory over the kings. He destroys the bronze doors and the iron bars; he gives Cyrus the treasures of darkness. Second Isaiah thus visualizes a political empire of Cyrus and not of Israel. Yahweh does all these things for his own sake: he brings Cyrus for the sake of his servant Jacob-Israel (v 4) who takes birth from Yahweh; he does it for the diffusion of monotheism in the whole world (v 6). The newborn servant is the one to bring the teaching/rule of Yahweh to the ends of the earth (42.4)

16) 47.1-15 (1, 5-6, 8-10, 12)

רְדִי וּשְׁבִי עַל־עָפָר בְּתוּלַת בַּת־בָּבֶל 1
שְׁבִי־לָאָרֶץ אֵין־כִּסֵּא בַּת־כַּשְׂדִּים
כִּי לֹא תוֹסִיפִי יִקְרְאוּ־לָךְ רַכָּה וַעֲנֻגָּה

....

שְׁבִי דוּמָם וּבֹאִי בַחֹשֶׁךְ בַּת־כַּשְׂדִּים 5
כִּי לֹא תוֹסִיפִי יִקְרְאוּ־לָךְ גְּבֶרֶת מַמְלָכוֹת
קָצַפְתִּי עַל־עַמִּי חִלַּלְתִּי נַחֲלָתִי 6

וָאֶתְּנֵם בְּיָדֵךְ לֹא־שַׂמְתְּ לָהֶם רַחֲמִים
עַל־זָקֵן הִכְבַּדְתְּ עֻלֵּךְ מְאֹד

....

8 וְעַתָּה שִׁמְעִי־זֹאת עֲדִינָה הַיּוֹשֶׁבֶת לָבֶטַח
הָאֹמְרָה בִּלְבָבָהּ אֲנִי וְאַפְסִי עוֹד
לֹא אֵשֵׁב אַלְמָנָה וְלֹא אֵדַע שְׁכוֹל
9 וְתָבֹאנָה לָּךְ שְׁתֵּי־אֵלֶּה רֶגַע בְּיוֹם אֶחָד
שְׁכוֹל וְאַלְמֹן כְּתֻמָּם בָּאוּ עָלַיִךְ
בְּרֹב כְּשָׁפַיִךְ בְּעָצְמַת חֲבָרַיִךְ מְאֹד
10 וַתִּבְטְחִי בְרָעָתֵךְ אָמַרְתְּ אֵין רֹאָנִי
חָכְמָתֵךְ וְדַעְתֵּךְ הִיא שׁוֹבְבָתֶךְ
וַתֹּאמְרִי בְלִבֵּךְ אֲנִי וְאַפְסִי עוֹד

....

12 עִמְדִי־נָא בַחֲבָרַיִךְ וּבְרֹב כְּשָׁפַיִךְ בַּאֲשֶׁר יָגַעַתְּ מִנְּעוּרָיִךְ
אוּלַי תּוּכְלִי הוֹעִיל אוּלַי תַּעֲרוֹצִי

1 Come down and sit in the dust, O virgin daughter of Babylon;

sit on the ground without a throne, O daughter of the Chaldeans! for you shall no more be called tender and delicate

....

5 Sit in silence, and go into darkness, O daughter of the Chaldeans;

For you shall no more be called the mistress of kingdoms

6 I was angry with my people, I profaned my heritage;

I gave them into your hand, you showed them no mercy;

on the elderly you laid your yoke very heavily.

....

8 Now therefore hear this, you (Babylon) lover of pleasures, who sit securely,

Who say in your heart, "*I am, and there is no one besides me*; I shall not sit as a widow or know the loss of children":
9 These two things shall come to you in a moment, in one day;
the loss of children and widowhood have come upon you
in full measure, in spite of your many sorceries and the great power of your enchantments.
10 You felt secure in your wickedness; you said, "No one sees me";
Your wisdom and your knowledge led you astray, and you said in your heart, "*I am, and there is no one besides me.*"

....

12 Stand fast in your enchantments and your many sorceries with which you have labored from your youth;
Perhaps you may be able to succeed … inspire terror.

Even though the prophet speaks great things about Yahweh, in the eyes of the exiles, Babylonian empire is still the most superior power. In Is 47.1-15, therefore, Yahweh summons Babylon to judgment; he lists her iniquities, and accuses her for pretending to be the superior power. Yahweh declares that it was he who gave up his people in the hands of Babylon (v 6); it was not his failure. He also challenges Babylon to save herself with the help of her gods if she can and inspire terror against Yahweh if it is in her capacity (v 12). Babylon, the great empire that boasted to have destroyed the kingdom of Yahweh, is now unable to escape from the wrath of Yahweh: as he once sent Judah into slavery, now he sends Babylon away (vv 1, 5; cf. also 48.14).

17) 48.20-21

20 צְאוּ מִבָּבֶל בִּרְחוּ מִכַּשְׂדִּים בְּקוֹל רִנָּה הַגִּידוּ
הַשְׁמִיעוּ זֹאת הוֹצִיאוּהָ עַד־קְצֵה הָאָרֶץ
אִמְרוּ גָּאַל יְהוָה עַבְדּוֹ יַעֲקֹב
21 וְלֹא צָמְאוּ בָּחֳרָבוֹת הוֹלִיכָם מַיִם מִצּוּר הִזִּיל לָמוֹ
וַיִּבְקַע־צוּר וַיָּזֻבוּ מָיִם

[20] Go forth from Babylon, flee from Chaldea, declare this with a shout of joy,
proclaim it, send it forth to the end of the earth;
say, "Yahweh has redeemed *his servant Jacob*!"
[21] They did not thirst when he led them through the ruins; he made water flow for them from the rock;
He cleft the rock and the water gushed out.

If Yahweh is going to take vengeance on Babylon, his servant - mandate - should flee from that place of destruction. In this servant passage ("Yahweh has redeemed his servant Jacob"), the servant is commanded to return from Babylon. The servant should go out from Babylon and announce that Yahweh has redeemed his servant. The second verse alludes to the exodus tradition of Israel by recalling the miraculous flowing of water in the desert (Num 20.1-13; Deut 8.15; Ps 78.15; 114.8); thus the prophet is calling for a second exodus which implies their rebirth for monotheism (v 21).

18) 49.1-6

שִׁמְעוּ אִיִּים אֵלַי וְהַקְשִׁיבוּ לְאֻמִּים מֵרָחוֹק 1
יְהוָה מִבֶּטֶן קְרָאָנִי מִמְּעֵי אִמִּי הִזְכִּיר שְׁמִי
וַיָּשֶׂם פִּי כְּחֶרֶב חַדָּה בְּצֵל יָדוֹ הֶחְבִּיאָנִי 2
וַיְשִׂימֵנִי לְחֵץ בָּרוּר בְּאַשְׁפָּתוֹ הִסְתִּירָנִי
וַיֹּאמֶר לִי עַבְדִּי־אָתָּה יִשְׂרָאֵל אֲשֶׁר־בְּךָ אֶתְפָּאָר 3
וַאֲנִי אָמַרְתִּי לְרִיק יָגַעְתִּי לְתֹהוּ וְהֶבֶל כֹּחִי כִלֵּיתִי 4
אָכֵן מִשְׁפָּטִי אֶת־יְהוָה וּפְעֻלָּתִי אֶת־אֱלֹהָי
וְעַתָּה אָמַר יְהוָה יֹצְרִי מִבֶּטֶן לְעֶבֶד לוֹ 5
לְשׁוֹבֵב יַעֲקֹב אֵלָיו יִשְׂרָאֵל לוֹ יֵאָסֵף
וְאֶכָּבֵד בְּעֵינֵי יְהוָה וֵאלֹהַי הָיָה עֻזִּי
וַיֹּאמֶר נָקֵל מִהְיוֹתְךָ לִי עֶבֶד לְהָקִים אֶת־שִׁבְטֵי יַעֲקֹב 6
וּנְצוּרֵי יִשְׂרָאֵל לְהָשִׁיב וּנְתַתִּיךָ לְאוֹר גּוֹיִם
לִהְיוֹת יְשׁוּעָתִי עַד־קְצֵה הָאָרֶץ

1 Listen to me, O coastlands, and hearken, you peoples from afar.

Yahweh called me *from the womb* from the body of my mother he made mention of my name.

2 He made my mouth like a *sharp sword*, in the shadow of his hand he hid me;

He made me a polished arrow, in his quiver he hid me away.

3 He said to me, "*You are my servant, Israel, in whom I will be glorified.*"

4 But I said, "I have labored in vain, I have spent my strength for nothing and vanity;

Yet surely my teaching (*mišpāṭî*) is Yahweh, and my recompense with my God."

5 And now Yahweh said, *who formed me from the womb to be his servant*,

to bring Jacob back to him, and that Israel will be gathered to him,

so that I will be honored in the eyes of Yahweh, and my God has become my strength

6 He said: "you are too little to be *my servant* to raise up the tribes of Jacob

and to restore the preserved of Israel, *but I will give you as a light to the nations*,

That my salvation may reach to the end of the earth."

This is the so-called 'second servant song.' Also in this text, even though metaphorical, the figure of Yahweh is that of a warrior who fights with a sharp sword, while hiding his polished arrow in his quiver. At the same time, the prophet presents himself as the model of true servanthood to which the exilic Israel is called ("He said to me, 'You are my servant, Israel, in whom I will be glorified," v 3). Through this verse, the servant is specified as that Israel in whom Yahweh will be glorified. This text thus makes a distinction between the servant Israel and the others (vv 5-6). It also links the servanthood of Israel with a promise: the servant will be made a light of salvation to the nations.

Yahweh, the warrior, formed the servant (Israel, v 3) in the womb (עֶבֶד, בֶּטֶן, יצר; 49.1, 5; see also 44.1, 21), and made his mouth like a sharp sword in order to destroy the mountains (49.2; 41.15). In 42.1-4 Yahweh announced that his servant would bring his rule / teaching to the *ends of the earth* (42.4); now the prophet-servant calls the *isles and nations* (49.1), and announces them that Yahweh called him from the womb, made his mouth like a sharp sword (כְּחֶרֶב חַדָּה), and hid him (חבא) in the shadow of his hand. We have already seen that the rule of Yahweh is not a political one; rather, it is a spiritual empire in which all proclaim Yahweh as the only God; the sword of Yahweh to establish this great empire is the sharp tongue of the servant. The universal empire of Yahweh will be the result of the teaching of this servant (his *mišpāt*).

The teaching of Yahweh is monotheism, which is the light of redemption to the nations (cf. 45.22). This is the sharp sword used by the servant (cf. also 41.10-16). At this point it is noteworthy to remember that the Bible often employs the language of violence when it announces monotheism. In fact, according to the research of scholars like J. Assmann, O. Keel, and B. Lang, the language of violence used by biblical monotheism comes from Mesopotamian political treaties, viz., it was the language used in the treaties that the Assyrian emperors made with their vassal kings.[127] Since Second Isaiah gives the most detailed treaties on Monotheism, it is probable that the Isaianic theology, that takes the ancient Near Eastern treaties as a basic metaphor, had exerted its influence on the redaction of many of these biblical books.

---

[127] Cf. for example, Esarhaddon's treaty with Baal, king of Tyre; cf. S. Parpola and K. Watanabe, *Neo-Assyrian Treaties and Loyalty Oaths* (SAA 2), Helsinki, University Press, 1987, 25 (line 18); Lang, "La violence au service de la religion: de quelques formes élémentaires d'agression dans la Bible," in *De la Violence*, ed. F. Héritier, Paris, Odile Jacob, 1996, 169-200; J. Assmann, *Monotheismus und die Sprache der Gewalt* (WVR 116), Wien, Picus, 2004, 26-30; O. Keel, "Monotheismus - ein göttlicher Makel? Über eine allzu bequeme Anklage," *NZZ* no. 254 of 30/31, October 2004, 68.

Why did Yahweh hide his servant in his shadow and in his quiver? It might be with the intention of using him like a weapon and shooting him in the suitable time. It thus alludes to an already existing monotheistic trend. Now this servant has to bring the tribes of Israel back to Yahweh (vv 5-6), and be a light of salvation to the nations (v 6). Bringing Israel back to Yahweh implies two things: (1) bringing them back to Zion from Babylon (48.21; 52.11-12), and (2) bringing them back to Yahweh from their idols, i.e., teaching them monotheism (44.6-22; 48.3-6). To be a light of salvation to the nations means to be a light of pro-Yahweh monotheism. Actually, according to Second Isaiah, all the nations have to come to Yahweh in order to be saved: "There is no other god besides me … turn to me and be saved, all the ends of the earth! For I am God, and there is no other" (45.21b-22).

Isaiah 49.1-6 on the one hand confirms that the servant is Israel; on the other hand this text specifies this servant Israel as that part of Israel in whom Yahweh will be glorified, i.e., those Israelites who accept Yahweh as the only God (49.3; cf. 42.8; 48.11).

That means that exilic Israel is composed of two groups: (a) 'the servant Israel' who already operates as a polished arrow in the hands of Yahweh and (b) the other part of Israel, that still needs a return to Yahweh (they are still blind; 49.5-6). The former is a very small part of Israel ("you are too little to be my servant," v 6) that has been loyal to Yahweh and has been trying to bring the house of Israel back to Yahweh, but up to now without much success (49.4). Yahweh, however, has made this servant even a light to the nations in order to bring his salvation to the ends of the earth (49.6). That means that the insignificant but faithful servant has become an important instrument -- a sharp sword and a polished arrow -- in the hands of the universal and mighty warrior.

19) 49.7

כֹּה אָמַר־יְהוָה גֹּאֵל יִשְׂרָאֵל קְדוֹשׁוֹ
לִבְזֹה־נֶפֶשׁ לִמְתָעֵב גּוֹי לְעֶבֶד מֹשְׁלִים
מְלָכִים יִרְאוּ וָקָמוּ שָׂרִים וְיִשְׁתַּחֲווּ
לְמַעַן יְהוָה אֲשֶׁר נֶאֱמָן קְדֹשׁ יִשְׂרָאֵל וַיִּבְחָרֶךָּ

Thus said Yahweh, the Redeemer of Israel and his Holy One,
To one deeply despised, abhorred by the nations, *the servant of rulers*:
"*Kings shall see and shall arise princes* and they shall prostrate themselves;
Because of Yahweh, who is faithful, the Holy One of Israel, who has chosen you.

Up to now Israel has been the servant (vassal) of the earthly rulers; however, now onwards they are going to be the servant of the mightiest ruler - Yahweh. This text thus adds another point to the promised glory. The figure of Yahweh envisaged is that of the most powerful emperor before whom all the kings and princess will stand up and prostrate; he now chooses Israel as his servant (49.7); in fact, he remains always faithful; he has not rejected them. The exiles, by contrast, had enough reasons to doubt about the announced faithfulness of Yahweh and his superior power. The prophet answers this question in the following text.

20) 49.22-26

22 כֹּה־אָמַר אֲדֹנָי יְהוִה
הִנֵּה אֶשָּׂא אֶל־גּוֹיִם יָדִי וְאֶל־עַמִּים אָרִים נִסִּי
וְהֵבִיאוּ בָנַיִךְ בְּחֹצֶן וּבְנֹתַיִךְ עַל־כָּתֵף תִּנָּשֶׂאנָה
23 וְהָיוּ מְלָכִים אֹמְנַיִךְ וְשָׂרוֹתֵיהֶם מֵינִיקֹתַיִךְ
אַפַּיִם אֶרֶץ יִשְׁתַּחֲווּ לָךְ וַעֲפַר רַגְלַיִךְ יְלַחֵכוּ
וְיָדַעַתְּ כִּי־אֲנִי יְהוָה אֲשֶׁר לֹא־יֵבֹשׁוּ קֹוָי
24 הֲיֻקַּח מִגִּבּוֹר מַלְקוֹחַ וְאִם־שְׁבִי צַדִּיק יִמָּלֵט
25 כִּי־כֹה אָמַר יְהוָה
גַּם־שְׁבִי גִבּוֹר יֻקָּח וּמַלְקוֹחַ עָרִיץ יִמָּלֵט
וְאֶת־יְרִיבֵךְ אָנֹכִי אָרִיב וְאֶת־בָּנַיִךְ אָנֹכִי אוֹשִׁיעַ
26 וְהַאֲכַלְתִּי אֶת־מוֹנַיִךְ אֶת־בְּשָׂרָם וְכֶעָסִיס דָּמָם יִשְׁכָּרוּן
וְיָדְעוּ כָל־בָּשָׂר כִּי אֲנִי יְהוָה מוֹשִׁיעֵךְ וְגֹאֲלֵךְ אֲבִיר יַעֲקֹב

22 Thus said Yahweh:

"Behold, *I will lift up my arm to the nations, and raise my signal to the people*s;

And they shall bring your sons in their bosom, and your daughters shall be carried on their shoulders.

23 *Kings shall be your foster fathers, and their queens your nursing mothers.*

With *their faces to the ground they shall bow down to you, and lick the dust of your feet.*

Then you will know that *I am Yahweh*; those who wait for me shall not be put to shame."

24 Can the prey be taken from the mighty, or the captives of a tyrant be rescued?

25 Surely, thus said Yahweh:

"*Even the captives of the mighty shall be taken, and the prey of the tyrant be rescued*,

For I will contend with those who contend with you, and I will save your children.
26 *I will make your oppressors eat their own flesh*, and they shall be drunk with their own blood as with wine.
Then all flesh shall know that *I am Yahweh* your savior, and your redeemer, *the mighty one* of Jacob."

In the previous text, the prophet declared that kings and princes would prostrate before Yahweh (49.7). Elucidating this point further here he says that Yahweh will lift up his arm to the nations and they will bring his exiles back. The kings and queens will also prostrate before Israel (the mandate of Yahweh) and lick the dust on their feet. This claim of Yahweh of having universal authority appears to the exiles only as a prophetic imagination because the exiles in Babylon are still like those who are trapped in holes (42.22). It makes the people ask the following question: "Can the prey be taken from the mighty, or the captives of a tyrant be rescued?" (v 24).

Before this relentless skepticism, the prophet affirms that Yahweh is the *great warrior* and he will take the prey out of the hands of the mighty. He is a warrior who fiercely fights for his servant. Through the present redemptive act, Yahweh will make them - both Israel and the nation - known that *he is Yahweh* (vv 23, 26): in Second Isaiah in fact 'Yahweh' is the name of the only God (45.18). That means that through the present redemption of Israel, Yahweh is going to teach both Israel and the nations that he is only God. In other words, the purpose of the actins of Yahweh as a warrior-emperor is the establishment of monotheism.

21) 50.4-11

אֲדֹנָי יְהוִה נָתַן לִי לְשׁוֹן לִמּוּדִים 4
לָדַעַת לָעוּת אֶת־יָעֵף דָּבָר יָעִיר
בַּבֹּקֶר בַּבֹּקֶר יָעִיר לִי אֹזֶן לִשְׁמֹעַ כַּלִּמּוּדִים
אֲדֹנָי יְהוִה פָּתַח־לִי אֹזֶן 5
וְאָנֹכִי לֹא מָרִיתִי אָחוֹר לֹא נְסוּגֹתִי
גֵּוִי נָתַתִּי לְמַכִּים וּלְחָיַי לְמֹרְטִים 6
פָּנַי לֹא הִסְתַּרְתִּי מִכְּלִמּוֹת וָרֹק
וַאדֹנָי יְהוִה יַעֲזָר־לִי עַל־כֵּן לֹא נִכְלָמְתִּי 7
עַל־כֵּן שַׂמְתִּי פָנַי כַּחַלָּמִישׁ וָאֵדַע כִּי־לֹא אֵבוֹשׁ
קָרוֹב מַצְדִּיקִי מִי־יָרִיב אִתִּי 8
נַעַמְדָה יָּחַד מִי־בַעַל מִשְׁפָּטִי יִגַּשׁ אֵלָי
הֵן אֲדֹנָי יְהוִה יַעֲזָר־לִי מִי־הוּא יַרְשִׁיעֵנִי 9
הֵן כֻּלָּם כַּבֶּגֶד יִבְלוּ עָשׁ יֹאכְלֵם
מִי בָכֶם יְרֵא יְהוָה שֹׁמֵעַ בְּקוֹל עַבְדּוֹ 10
אֲשֶׁר הָלַךְ חֲשֵׁכִים וְאֵין נֹגַהּ לוֹ
יִבְטַח בְּשֵׁם יְהוָה וְיִשָּׁעֵן בֵּאלֹהָיו
הֵן כֻּלְּכֶם קֹדְחֵי אֵשׁ מְאַזְּרֵי זִיקוֹת 11
לְכוּ בְּאוּר אֶשְׁכֶם וּבְזִיקוֹת בִּעַרְתֶּם
מִיָּדִי הָיְתָה־זֹּאת לָכֶם לְמַעֲצֵבָה תִּשְׁכָּבוּן

4 Lord Yahweh has given me *the tongue of those who are taught*,
that I may know how to sustain with a word him that is weary.
Morning by morning he wakens, *he wakens my ear to hear as those who are taught*.
5 Lord Yahweh has opened my ear,
And *I was not rebellious*, I turned not backward.
6 I gave my back to the smiters, and my cheeks to those who

pulled out the beard;
I hid not my face from shame and spitting.
7 And the Lord Yahweh will help me; therefore I have not been confounded;
therefore I have set my face like a flint, and I know that I shall not be put to shame;
8 *he who redeems me is near.* Who will contend with me? Let us stand up together.
Who will contend with my teaching (*mišpātî*)? Let him come near to me.
9 Behold, the Lord Yahweh will help me; who will declare me guilty?
Behold, all of them will wear out like a garment; the moth will eat them up.
10 Who among you fears Yahweh and obeys the voice of *his servant*,
who walked in darkness and had no light, let him trust in the name of Yahweh and rely upon his God?
11 Behold, all you who kindle a fire, who set brands alight!
(you) walk in the flame of your fire, and in the flares which you have kindled!
This happened to you from my hand: you shall lie down in torment.

This text, which contains the so-called ‘third servant song’ (vv 4-9) can be taken as a servant passage because v 10 qualifies the speaker of vv 4-9 as the servant of Yahweh. The song may be seen as the song of the obedient servant who appeared in 49.1-6 for three reasons: (a) here the speaker demonstrates his readiness to hear the word of Yahweh ("Morning by morning he ... wakens my ear to hear as those who are taught," 50.4); Yahweh opened his ear and he did not rebel (50.5; against 42.19); he also narrates the difficulties that he had to encounter as the result of his faithfulness to Yahweh (v 6, 10b; compare 49.4); (b) he hopes that he will be redeemed by his God (50.8; compare 49.4b) and he knows (ידע) that he will not be put to shame (בוש, 50.7; compare 49.4); (c) he has a tongue like one who is taught ("Lord Yahweh has given me the tongue of those who are taught," 50.4; compare 49.2cd, that speaks about a tongue like a sharp sword), and thus he knows (ידע) how to sustain with a word him that is weary (50.4).

The text thus seems to be the words of the servant who already undergoes the regeneration. In order to undergo this process of regeneration, Israel should have the readiness to obtain knowledge from Yahweh (vv 4-5), the patience to wait for Yahweh (vv 7-8), and the courage to withstand against the popular notions (v 7). They also need a firm hope in the redemption of Yahweh (v 7).

At the end of this text, the prophet, who is part of the servant-Israel, makes a final call to the other group of Israel to follow the way of Yahweh and to believe in him: "Who among you fears Yahweh ... let him trust in the name of Yahweh ... Behold, all you who kindle a fire ... walk in the flame of your fire" (v 10-11). These harsh words of the servant seem to recall one of the disgraceful events in the exodus tradition of Israel. According to Num 16, during the exodus journey, 250 Israelites rebelled against the teaching of Moses, the servant of Yahweh. They argued that the entire congregation was holy to Yahweh.

In order to prove their case and to show their equality with Moses, they took their censer, put fire in it, laid incense on the fire, and then stood at the entrance of the tent of meeting with Moses and Aaron. Yahweh then told Moses and Aaron to move away from these wicked men so that he might consume them in a moment (vv 20-21). These rebels faced a disastrous death; they were destroyed because of their own fire (v 18).

The Isaianic poem seems to recall this terrible event (Num 16) and allude to the servanthood of Moses because of the following elements: (a) its literary context recalls the exodus tradition of Israel (50.2-3); (b) like Moses, Isaianic servant speaks with Yahweh and learns from him (v 4); (c) the poem speaks about the opposition that the servant faced, an opposition comparable to that one Moses faced (vv 6-8); (d) like Moses, the servant is accused of being guilty by the rebels (v 9); (e) like Moses, he calls his hearers to believe in Yahweh (v 10); (f) like Moses, he declares that the non believers will be destroyed in the fire that they themselves have kindled (v 11). See the other allusions to Moses in the poem:

Ref. Is	Isaianic servant of Yahweh	Moses, the servant of Yahweh	Ref.
50.4-5	He has a *tongue* to teach the weary and he without rebellion hears Yahweh's word every morning	He complained that he was not eloquent; Yahweh assured him a good *tongue* , taught him what is to be said	Ex 4.10-12

50.4-5	The servant undergoes humiliation; he has hope in Yahweh	Moses underwent humiliating experiences; he was proved right by Yahweh	Num 16.1-35
50.4, 10	He was taught by Yahweh; he was with Yahweh in darkness	Moses was taught the law by Yahweh in darkness on Mt Sinai	Deut 4.11; 5.22-23
50.10-11	He makes a final call to believe in Yahweh as the only God and threatens destruction if they disobey	Moses after an idolatrous event called Israel to believe in Yahweh as their God and destroyed the non-believing	Ex 32.26

What kind of discipline was this new servant undergoing (50.4-5)? The literary and historical contexts (Is 40-53) show that it was a discipline of monotheism. Pre-exilic prophets, especially the Yahweh-alonists, warned Israel of destruction, if they did not go away from their idols (Jer 25.1-11). The transgression of Israel brought destruction to Zion (50.1-3; see also 42.24; 43.27-28). This destruction taught the servant that Yahweh was in control of the history of Israel because in the destruction the prophetic words of Yahweh were fulfilled. The servant, therefore, believed in Yahweh. He was taught by Yahweh, day by day (vv 4-5), and thus he was undergoing the regeneration. He had a word that could sustain the weary (40.27-31; 49.1-6, 8-21, 22-26); every day he had his eyes open and he was always learning (contrast 42.18-19). He took exile as a period of learning and rebirth.

After encouraging his hearers based on the example of his own faith, the servant makes his climactic call to the skeptics to give heed to his message: "Who among you fears Yahweh and obeys the voice of his servant, who walked in darkness and had no light, let him believe in the name of Yahweh so that he can rely upon his God?" (v 10). That means, now, the exilic servant of Yahweh (the new Moses) is making the final call to the exiles to return to Zion (the Promised Land) which is also followed by a final threat of destruction if they fail to follow this call: "behold all of them will wear out like a garment; the moth will eat them up" (v 9, i.e., they will slowly die out); "Behold, all you who kindle a fire, who set brands alight! Walk in the flame of your fire; … you shall lie down in torment" (v 11). Since Yahweh helps his servant, his challengers will be worn out like a garment and will be eaten up by moth. After this final call, in fact, the skeptical group is no more addressed by the prophet.

22) 51.1-3

שִׁמְעוּ אֵלַי רֹדְפֵי צֶדֶק מְבַקְשֵׁי יְהוָה 1
הַבִּיטוּ אֶל־צוּר חֻצַּבְתֶּם וְאֶל־מַקֶּבֶת בּוֹר נֻקַּרְתֶּם
הַבִּיטוּ אֶל־אַבְרָהָם אֲבִיכֶם וְאֶל־שָׂרָה תְּחוֹלֶלְכֶם 2
כִּי־אֶחָד קְרָאתִיו וַאֲבָרְכֵהוּ וְאַרְבֵּהוּ
כִּי־נִחַם יְהוָה צִיּוֹן נִחַם כָּל־חָרְבֹתֶיהָ 3
וַיָּשֶׂם מִדְבָּרָהּ כְּעֵדֶן וְעַרְבָתָהּ כְּגַן־יְהוָה
שָׂשׂוֹן וְשִׂמְחָה יִמָּצֵא בָהּ תּוֹדָה וְקוֹל זִמְרָה

[1] "Hearken to me, you who pursue redemption, you who seek Yahweh;
look to the rock from which you were hewn, and to the quarry from which you were digged.
[2] Look to Abraham your father and to Sarah who bore you;
for when he was but one I called him, and I blessed him and made him many.
[3] For Yahweh has comforted Zion; he has comforted all her waste places,
he made her wilderness like Eden, her desert like the garden of Yahweh;
joy and gladness will be found in her, thanksgiving and the voice of song.

According to the first servant text, the servant-Israel is defined as the offspring of Abraham; there Yahweh announces that he has gathered this Israel from the ends of the earth in order to tell him that he is Yahweh's servant (41.8-9). If the servant is the offspring of Abraham, then 51.1-3 can be considered as a servant passage even though the word servant (*'ebed*) does not appear there.[128] In this text, Yahweh addresses those who seek redemption (*ṣedeq*) and Yahweh: "Hearken to me, you who pursue redemption, you who seek Yahweh," (v 51.1). In exile, only those who were convinced of the true divinity of Yahweh (those who accepted servanthood) sought Yahweh and his redemption (49.4; 50.8). Yahweh now assures them the restoration of Zion like the Garden

[128] According to Duhm (*Das Buch*, 311) Is 50.4-9 is a servant song; however, the noun *'ebed* does not appear there.

of Eden; by recalling the experience of Abraham and Sarah, he is assuring an eternal nation to his servant.

As already mentioned more than once, the call to be the servant of Yahweh is accompanied by a promise of a glorious future. The text appeals to the experience of Abraham in order to promise the restoration of the Promised Land. The ruins of Zion are similar to Abraham who was an old man, and like Sarah who was barren; but Yahweh called Abraham, blessed him and increased him (v 2).

Abraham was taken first from Ur and later from Haran (Gen 11.31-12.4); he was delivered from Egypt and Gerar. If Yahweh was capable of bringing a people from the old Abraham and barren Sarah, and delivering them from the mighty kings of the time, he shall surely be able to deliver Israel from Babylon. If he was able to make a nation from this old and infertile couple, how much more can he make out of this small group of exiles who want to go to Zion? The marvelous Garden of Eden was not a work of human hands. If Yahweh did such amazing things in the past, why should his people doubt the new message of restoration?

23) 51.4-5

4 הַקְשִׁיבוּ אֵלַי עַמִּי וּלְאוּמִּי אֵלַי הַאֲזִינוּ
כִּי תוֹרָה מֵאִתִּי תֵצֵא וּמִשְׁפָּטִי לְאוֹר עַמִּים אַרְגִּיעַ
5 קָרוֹב צִדְקִי יָצָא יִשְׁעִי וּזְרֹעַי עַמִּים יִשְׁפֹּטוּ
אֵלַי אִיִּים יְקַוּוּ וְאֶל־זְרֹעִי יְיַחֵלוּן

[4] "Listen to me, my people, and give ear to me, my nation;
for teaching (*tôrāh*) will go forth from me and *I will make rest my rule* (*mišpāt*) *for a light to the peoples*.
[5] My deliverance is near, my salvation has gone forth, and *my arms will rule* (*špt*) *the peoples*;
coastlands wait for me, and for *my arm* they hope.

After the assurances of restoration given in the previous text, the present text presents Yahweh once again as the universal ruler and law giver. His teaching and arm will rule the nations. According to the vision of Second Isaiah, the restored city of Yahweh will be the centre of monotheism; it will be the cosmic centre from which Yahweh will rule the nations (cf. 51.3; 45.13, 14). In the following verses Yahweh will affirm that the redemption brought by him will last for ever: "my salvation will be for ever, and my deliverance will never be ended" (vv 6-8). If Yahweh is an everlasting God, the redemption realized by him can also transcend place and time (cf. 40.22, 28).

24) 52.7-10

7 מַה־נָּאווּ עַל־הֶהָרִים רַגְלֵי מְבַשֵּׂר
מַשְׁמִיעַ שָׁלוֹם מְבַשֵּׂר טוֹב מַשְׁמִיעַ יְשׁוּעָה
אֹמֵר לְצִיּוֹן מָלַךְ אֱלֹהָיִךְ
8 קוֹל צֹפַיִךְ נָשְׂאוּ קוֹל יַחְדָּו יְרַנֵּנוּ
כִּי עַיִן בְּעַיִן יִרְאוּ בְּשׁוּב יְהוָה צִיּוֹן
9 פִּצְחוּ רַנְּנוּ יַחְדָּו חָרְבוֹת יְרוּשָׁלִָם
כִּי־נִחַם יְהוָה עַמּוֹ גָּאַל יְרוּשָׁלִָם
10 חָשַׂף יְהוָה אֶת־זְרוֹעַ קָדְשׁוֹ לְעֵינֵי כָּל־הַגּוֹיִם
וְרָאוּ כָּל־אַפְסֵי־אָרֶץ אֵת יְשׁוּעַת אֱלֹהֵינוּ

[7] How beautiful upon the mountains are the feet of him who brings good tidings,
who proclaim peace, who brings good news, who proclaims salvation,
who says to Zion, "*Your God reigns*."
[8] Hark, your watchmen lift up their voice, together they sing for joy;
for eye to eye they see the return of Yahweh to Zion.
[9] Break forth together into singing, you waste places of Jerusalem;
for Yahweh has comforted his people, he has redeemed Jerusalem.
[10] Yahweh has *bared his holy arm* before the eyes of *all the nations*; all the ends of the earth shall see the salvation of our God.

In the literary context (51.9), the prophet has already prayed to the arm of Yahweh to show its might: "Awake, awake, put on strength, O arm of Yahweh; awake, as in the days of old ... was it not you that cut Rahab in pieces that pierced the dragon?" In the present verse, which is the last Isaianic text that speaks about the universal power of Yahweh, he declares that Yahweh has already shown his power before the nations. This prompts the prophet-servant to cry out to the exiles to make a new exodus from Babylon to Zion: "Depart, depart, go out from there! *Touch no unclean thing* (טָמֵא)! Come out from it; *purify yourselves*, you who bear the vessels of Yahweh for you shall not leave in haste or go in flight; for Yahweh will go before you, the God of Israel will be your rear guard." (52.11-12).

Since Yahweh is the universal and the most powerful emperor they don't have to be in a hurry or to flee. Yahweh will go before them; however, they all should be pure in such a way to follow Yahweh and to carry his vessels. The nominal adjective *ṭame'* (טָמֵא) refers to the uncleanness that results either from the contact with the dead bodies or from idolatry that is labeled as adultery. This is thus the final call to leave Babylon, the land of idolatry and death. The Yahweh-alone party used to depict idolatry as impurity.[129]

25) 52.13-53.12

13 הִנֵּה יַשְׂכִּיל עַבְדִּי יָרוּם וְנִשָּׂא וְגָבַהּ מְאֹד
14 כַּאֲשֶׁר שָׁמְמוּ עָלֶיךָ רַבִּים
כֵּן־מִשְׁחַת מֵאִישׁ מַרְאֵהוּ וְתֹאֲרוֹ מִבְּנֵי אָדָם
15 כֵּן יַזֶּה גּוֹיִם רַבִּים עָלָיו יִקְפְּצוּ מְלָכִים פִּיהֶם
כִּי אֲשֶׁר לֹא־סֻפַּר לָהֶם רָאוּ וַאֲשֶׁר לֹא־שָׁמְעוּ הִתְבּוֹנָנוּ
1 מִי הֶאֱמִין לִשְׁמֻעָתֵנוּ וּזְרוֹעַ יְהוָה עַל־מִי נִגְלָתָה
2 וַיַּעַל כַּיּוֹנֵק לְפָנָיו וְכַשֹּׁרֶשׁ מֵאֶרֶץ צִיָּה
לֹא־תֹאַר לוֹ וְלֹא הָדָר וְנִרְאֵהוּ וְלֹא־מַרְאֶה וְנֶחְמְדֵהוּ
3 נִבְזֶה וַחֲדַל אִישִׁים אִישׁ מַכְאֹבוֹת וִידוּעַ חֹלִי
וּכְמַסְתֵּר פָּנִים מִמֶּנּוּ נִבְזֶה וְלֹא חֲשַׁבְנֻהוּ
4 אָכֵן חֳלָיֵנוּ הוּא נָשָׂא וּמַכְאֹבֵינוּ סְבָלָם

---

[129] "I know Ephraim, and Israel is not hid from me; for now, O Ephraim, you have played the harlot; Israel has become unclean (נִטְמָא)" (Hos 5.3; cf. also 6.10); "How can you say, 'I am not defiled (לֹא נִטְמֵאתִי), I have not gone after the Baals'?" (Jer 2.23); "she (Ephraim) defiled herself (נִטְמָאָה) with all the idols of every one on whom she doted" (Ezek 23.7; see also vv 13, 17; 24.13; 43.7; Josh 22.19).

וַאֲנַחְנוּ חֲשַׁבְנֻהוּ נָגוּעַ מֻכֵּה אֱלֹהִים וּמְעֻנֶּה
5 וְהוּא מְחֹלָל מִפְּשָׁעֵנוּ מְדֻכָּא מֵעֲוֹנֹתֵינוּ
מוּסַר שְׁלוֹמֵנוּ עָלָיו וּבַחֲבֻרָתוֹ נִרְפָּא־לָנוּ
6 כֻּלָּנוּ כַּצֹּאן תָּעִינוּ אִישׁ לְדַרְכּוֹ פָּנִינוּ
וַיהוָה הִפְגִּיעַ בּוֹ אֵת עֲוֹן כֻּלָּנוּ
7 נִגַּשׂ וְהוּא נַעֲנֶה וְלֹא יִפְתַּח־פִּיו
כַּשֶּׂה לַטֶּבַח יוּבָל וּכְרָחֵל לִפְנֵי גֹזְזֶיהָ נֶאֱלָמָה וְלֹא יִפְתַּח פִּיו
8 מֵעֹצֶר וּמִמִּשְׁפָּט לֻקָּח וְאֶת־דּוֹרוֹ מִי יְשׂוֹחֵחַ
כִּי נִגְזַר מֵאֶרֶץ חַיִּים מִפֶּשַׁע עַמִּי נֶגַע לָמוֹ
9 וַיִּתֵּן אֶת־רְשָׁעִים קִבְרוֹ וְאֶת־עָשִׁיר בְּמֹתָיו
עַל לֹא־חָמָס עָשָׂה וְלֹא מִרְמָה בְּפִיו
10 וַיהוָה חָפֵץ דַּכְּאוֹ הֶחֱלִי אִם־תָּשִׂים אָשָׁם נַפְשׁוֹ
יִרְאֶה זֶרַע יַאֲרִיךְ יָמִים וְחֵפֶץ יְהוָה בְּיָדוֹ יִצְלָח
11 מֵעֲמַל נַפְשׁוֹ יִרְאֶה יִשְׂבָּע
בְּדַעְתּוֹ יַצְדִּיק צַדִּיק עַבְדִּי לָרַבִּים וַעֲוֹנֹתָם הוּא יִסְבֹּל
12 לָכֵן אֲחַלֶּק־לוֹ בָרַבִּים וְאֶת־עֲצוּמִים יְחַלֵּק שָׁלָל
תַּחַת אֲשֶׁר הֶעֱרָה לַמָּוֶת נַפְשׁוֹ וְאֶת־פֹּשְׁעִים נִמְנָה
וְהוּא חֵטְא־רַבִּים נָשָׂא וְלַפֹּשְׁעִים יַפְגִּיעַ

52.13 Behold, *my servant shall be wise*, he shall be exalted and lifted up, and shall be very high.

14 As many were astonished at him,

his appearance was so marred, beyond human semblance, and his form beyond that of the sons of men

15 so shall *he will sprinkle many nations*; *kings shall shut their mouths because of him*;

for that which has not been told them they have seen, and that which they have not heard they shall have understood.

53.1 Who has believed our account? And to whom has the *arm of Yahweh* been revealed?

2 For *he grew up before him like a young plant*, and like a

root out of dry ground;
he had no form or comeliness that we should look at him, and no beauty that we should desire him.

3 He was despised and rejected by men; a man of sorrows, and acquainted with grief;
and as one from whom men hide their faces; he was despised, and we esteemed him not.

4 Surely he has borne our griefs and carried our sorrows;
yet we esteemed him stricken, smitten by God, and afflicted.

5 But he was wounded for our transgressions, he was bruised for our iniquities;
upon him was the chastisement that made us whole, and with his stripes we are healed.

6 All we like sheep have gone astray; we have turned every one to his own way;
and Yahweh has laid on him the iniquity of us all.

7 He was oppressed, and he was afflicted, yet he opened not his mouth;
Like a lamb that is led to the slaughter, and like a sheep that before its shearers is dumb, so he opened not his mouth.

8 By the reason of oppression and rule of Yahweh (*mišpāt*)
he was taken away; and who will speak of his descendants?
he was cut off out of the land of the living, stricken for the transgression of my people?

9 He was given his grave with the wicked and with a rich man in his *deaths*,
although he had done no violence, and there was no deceit in his mouth.

10 Yet it was the will of Yahweh to bruise him; and cause
him to suffer; *if he will make himself an offering for sin, he shall see his offspring*;

he shall prolong his days and the will of Yahweh shall prosper in his hand;
11 he shall see the fruit of the travail of his soul and be satisfied;
b^{e}da'tô yaṣdîq ṣadîq 'abdî lârabîm and he shall bear their iniquities.
12 Therefore *I will divide him a portion with the great*, and he shall divide the spoil with the strong;
because he poured out his soul to death, and *was numbered with the transgressors*;
yet he bore the sin of many, and will make intercession for the transgressors.

This last servant passage is the so-called 'fourth servant song' in which the word servant (*'ebed*) appears in the beginning and at the end (52.13; 53.11). The similarity of this servant figure to Job has already been mentioned in the beginning of this discussion. As he presented his servant-ideal in 42.1-4, here, first Yahweh presents his obedient servant (52.13-15); then follows a comment by a group of people (53.1-11a) who seem to have followed the last call of the servant (50.10), and the poem concludes with another divine comment on his servant (11b-12).

Who is this servant, the one who suffers for others? (a) This is a servant who *will be* exalted by Yahweh (52.13); (b) he had no desirable form (v 14); (c) he *will sprinkle* many, and *nations* and *kings will wonder* about him because they will have seen and understood a new things (52.15; cf. 49.6; Ezek 36.25); (d) he grew up like a plant before Yahweh, and was formless like a *root out of the earth* (53.2); he had no human form due to the destruction; (e) he was despised by men (v 3; cf. 50.7); (f) however, he was suffering for the transgression of the people who walked in *their own ways* thinking that the servant was smitten by God (vv 4-6); (g) he was like a lamb brought to the slaughter, still he did not react; he was *removed from the land* of the living, and was *buried with the wicked* (vv 7-9); (h) he was taken for the rule of Yahweh (*mišpāt*); (i) all his sufferings *were according to the will of Yahweh* (v 10); (j) if he will submit his life (נֶפֶשׁ), *he will see offspring*, he will prolong days and the *plan of Yahweh will be accomplished* through him (v 10); (k) the servant *will* redeem many *by his knowledge* (*b^{e}da'tô yaṣdîq ṣadîq 'abdî*) and bear their iniquities (vv 11); (l) the servant interceded for *many* by offering his soul to death; therefore, *he will divide spoil with the mighty* (v 12).

The poem first speaks about the death and burial of the servant, then about his future life that will see his offspring and long days of life (vv 8-10); he will also divide the spoil with the mighty because he submitted his soul to death (v 12). Here, the first question is whether the text speaks about a real death of the servant or not.[130]

---

130 Some scholars suggest that the servant really died (cf. vv 7-8); Blenkinsopp (*Isaiah 40-55*, 354-56), for example, interprets the alleged afterlife of the servant in terms of his 'spiritual' presence among his followers who are the descendents (i.e., Second Isaiah is the servant in 53; in 49.1-6 and 50.4-9 he himself is the speaker; one of his disciples composed chapter 53). Isaiah 53, however, seems to employ metaphorical language similar to that is found in the lamentation psalms: Lam 3.54, for example, says אָמַרְתִּי נִגְזָרְתִּי "I have been cut off"; cf. Torrey, *The Second Isaiah*, 421; Whybray, *Isaiah 40-55*, 1981, 177.

If he will prolong his days through his suffering and will divide the spoil with the mighty, one cannot speak about the actual death of the servant; therefore, the alleged death and burial of the servant is only metaphorical. In addition, the text is speaking about the deaths (עָשִׁיר בְּמֹתָיו) and not about the death: one cannot die more than once.

Notably, the metaphor of afterlife was employed by the biblical authors of the exilic and post exilic period in order to depict the idea of the national restoration of Israel (cf. Ezek 37.1-14).[131] The reference to the death and resurrection of the servant seems to be an allusion to this idea, as it is confirmed by the conditional clause that follows the death: if the servant will submit his soul as an offering, he will see offspring and long days (v 10).

The death of the servant, therefore, is only metaphorical, a language similar to Jer 11.19; moreover, an

---

[131] In the exilic period, the Jewish concept on afterlife was not much developed. After death the person was thought to go to Sheol from where he would not ascend (Job 7.9). The dating of two biblical texts (Deut 32.39; 1Sam 2.6), in which one sees the idea of afterlife is alluded, is subject to dispute. The earliest description of an eschatological resurrection of the dead is found in Dan 12.1-2, a text composed during the time of the Antiochian persecutions (167-64 B.C.). In fact, the idea of immortality first began to appear in the Hellenistic Jewish literature (Wisdom of Solomon 3.1-10; 5.15-16) and then it was developed by Philo Judaeus; cf. D. Stern, "Afterlife Jewish Concepts," *EncyRel* I (1987), 120; R. H. Charles, *The Doctrine of a Future Life in Israel, Judaism and Christianity*. A Critical History, New York, Schocken Books, 1963; W. E. Nickelsburg, *Resurrection, Immortality, and Eternal Life in Inter-Testamental Judaism*, Cambridge, Harvard University, 1972. Josephus Flavius, *Jewish Antiquities*, 18.13-18; *The Jewish War*, 2.154-165; Acts 23.6-9.

analogous language is visible in Is 41.14 where the living Israelites in exile are addressed by the prophet as the *dead Israel* (מְתֵי יִשְׂרָאֵל): this text does not mean that the Israelites are dead. One can say that the servant was humiliated in such a way that his existence was comparable to that of a dead person (compare Job 3.20-26).

Yahweh had a plan that he wanted to achieve through the suffering of his servant: he wanted to reveal his arm to the nations (cf. 53.1: "to whom has the arm of Yahweh been revealed?"). In Second Isaiah, the arm of Yahweh implies his universal rule (cf. 40.10; 51.5, 9; 52.10). In order to realize this plan, Yahweh led his servant to that project (v 10). The servant, by silently undergoing the sufferings, up to now, succeeded in realizing this appointed task; however, the task is not yet complete. He should still (once again) submit his life (נֶפֶשׁ) as offering for the sins of others; then, *he will see offspring*, and will prolong his days and the *plan of Yahweh will fully be accomplished* (v 10). Yahweh will then glorify him (52.13).

The other speakers, who walked in their own ways (i.e., who did not obey Yahweh's commandments; cf. foot note 119), without understanding the plan of Yahweh, now perceive and recognize that the suffering of the servant has been the consequence of their transgression (53.5). The servant has been undergoing the suffering, but this mission is not yet complete. What is this yet unfinished plan of Yahweh that still demands self sacrifice from the servant ("if he will make himself an offering for sin," תָּשִׂים אָשָׁם נַפְשׁוֹ, v 10)?

In order to understand this poem, one should look into the metaphors here used by the prophet. One of the important metaphors employed is that of the sacrificial lambs of Day of Atonement (*Yom Kippur*; cf. Lev 16.1-28).

On this great annual feast/fast day, two lambs (one goat) were brought to the temple for the atonement liturgy. One was to be offered before Yahweh; this lamb would be slaughtered by the high priest; then the altar, temple, and people would be sprinkled with its blood so that all these would be purified from the impurities caused by the transgression of the people. The other lamb / goat (to Azazel) was intended to carry the sins of the people away from the city; the high priest would lay his hands on this goat and would confess over its head all the transgressions and sins of the people. This goat that now carries all the sins of the people would subsequently be lead to the desert, and it would die in the desert.

Isaiah 53.7b ("like a lamb that is led to the slaughter, and like a sheep that before its shearers is dumb") seems to allude to the image of the lamb designated for Yahweh that offers its blood as atonement for the sins of the people. Like this lamb of atonement, the servant was cut off from the land of the living even though he did not take upon himself the sacrifice voluntarily; but Yahweh imposed it on him (v 10); he was taken for the sake of the universal rule (*mišpāt*) of Yahweh (v 8). This allusion seems to be confirmed by 52.15 that speaks about a sprinkling (נָזָה; cf. Lev 16.14, 15, 19) achieved by means of the servant.

In 53.10b the goat designed to Azazel seems to be alluded: the noun *'āšām* (אָשָׁם) signifies a 'guilt offering,' the animal without blemish (Lev 5.19; 7.5; 14.21; 19.21). The exilic servant in Babylon is still expected ("if he will make himself an offering for sin," v 10) to offer his life like this goat by going away from the city (Babylon) to the desert of Zion. In this journey, he is carrying the sins of transgressions of the people.

The exiles had still in memory, the deportation of their kings and the valuable things of their temple and of the palace to Babylon (and Egypt) by the mighty emperors and their captains (2King 24.10-17). The Mesopotamian emperors also used to exalt their faithful vassals;[132] similarly, the servant of Emperor Yahweh, once his task is completed, *will be exalted* by his lord and he will divide the booty with the great (Is 52.13; 53.12).

Can this servant of Yahweh be defined rather clearly? From the holistic reading of Is 40-53, we already suggested that the servant is Israel, i.e., the obedient part of the community. Isaiah 40-53 specifies more than once that the servant (*'ebed* in singular) is Jacob-Israel (41.8; 44.1; 48.20; 49.3). All the Israelites, however, are not this suffering servant, because the last poem speaks about a community of Israelites who witnessed the suffering of the servant and who now recognizes the value of it which according to them is vicarious (53.3-6).

From the history of Israel, one knows that Ezekiel was one among the deportees; Daniel was also there when Cyrus conquered Babylon (cf. Dan 1.21; 6.29; 10.1). Second Isaiah lived in exile; there were of course similar other persons, and the disciples of these prophets; Deuteronomist theologians also lived there. That means that

---

[132] The Assyrian emperors, after having dedicated the captive gods to the chief god of their empire, shared the booty among the officialdom and royal cities; Cogan, *Imperialism*, 29, 48-49.

there was an obedient group that understood the plan of Yahweh (50.4-9); some texts in Second Isaiah show that the servant has a mission to the fellow exiles (49.3-5; 50.4; 53.5-6); In fact, Is 44.26 (cf. 42.18-19) equals the servant with the messengers of Yahweh. Actually, the Yahweh-alone party used to present the prophets of Yahweh as the servants of Yahweh (1King 14.18; 18.36; 2King 14.25; Jer 7.25; 25.4; 26.5; 29.19; 35.15; 44.4; Ezek 38.17; Zech 1.6; Dan 9.6, 10).

The servanthood of Israel seen as a call to be the messenger of monotheism indicates that the servant is the Yahweh-alone party. It began to grow before Yahweh like a small plant and was not a majority faction: "It grew up before him like a young plant" (cf. 53.2a); its work often appeared to be fruitless (49.4); it was uprooted and had no desirable form (53.2); not many gave heed to their message (cf. 53.1). They were innocent before Yahweh but were counted similar to others and were exiled (up-rooted/cut off). In the eyes of the people, they were people smitten by God (cf. Gen 18.25; footnote no 78). Even though they were just, Yahweh wanted to impose on them this suffering in order to execute his plan for the whole world (i.e., the establishment of monotheism; cf. 45.6). He was taken for *mišpāt*.

This plan was outlined in 42.1-4 (he will bring forth *mišpāt* to the nations); in order to execute this plan Yahweh himself led them to this exilic suffering. In Babylon, in a critical but international setting, this party became the witnesses of Yahweh's divinity by painstakingly preserving and reinterpreting their traditional faith in Yahweh (cf. 44.8; 50.4, 7).

Now, (by bringing Cyrus) Yahweh is asking them to go back from Babylon to the desert of Zion (cf. 51.3; 52.11-12) and thus bring this God-given mission to its fulfillment because Zion, according to the Yahweh-alone party, is the only right centre of the worship of Yahweh. It is by means of this return-journey of Yahweh with his chosen servant, that his glory is going to be manifested to the nations (cf. 40.5; 48.20; 51.11; 52.8, 11-12). He is going to "rule" the world from Zion (51.4). That seems to be the reason why the poem employs the metaphor of the lamb that sheds its blood for the exilic servant (52.13; 53.8) and the metaphor of the scapegoat for the same servant who is expected to go to Zion (53.10-12). Historically speaking, only those who were convinced (knew) of Yahweh as the only God could be courageous enough to sacrifice the security and prosperity offered by the great empire in Babylon and to proceed to the ruins of Zion.

It is through the *obedient submission to this plan of Yahweh* and through his *knowledge about Yahweh as the only God* that he is going to gain longevity and progeny (53.10-11). The expression *b^eda'tô* (בְּדַעְתּוֹ) is said to be the most unclear word in the text.[133] The word, however,

[133] J. A. Emerton ("A Consideration of Some Alleged Meanings of ידע in Hebrew," *JSS* 15 [1970], 145-188) presents a long list of interpretations given to this biblical term by ancient versions, commentators throughout the centuries, and by a good number modern scholars. For example, W. D. Thomas ("A Consideration of Isaiah liii in the Light of Recent Textual and Philological Study," *ETL* 44 [1968], 79-86; "The root ידע in Hebrew," *JTS* 35 [1934], 298-306) and G. R. Driver ("Linguistic and Textual Problems: Isaiah XL-LXVI," *JTS* 36 [1935], 396-406) interpret it as 'to

can be translated as 'knowledge' in the context of Is 40-53: it is through his knowledge that the servant is going to redeem many.

What is this knowledge through which the servant redeems many? The verb יָדַע (to know) appears altogether 37 times - 34 verses - in Is 40-53 (40.13, 14, 21, 28; 41.20, 22, 23, 26; 42.16[2x], 25; 43.10, 19; 44.8, 9, 18; 45.3, 4, 5, 6, 20; 47.8, 11 [2x], 13; 48.4, 6, 7, 8 [2x]; 49.23, 26; 50.4, 7; 51.7; 52.6; 53.3), and its substantive five times (40.14; 44.19, 25; 47.10; 53.11). The number of occurrences shows the importance of this word to Second Isaiah. All the four occurrences of the substantive (excluding 53.11) refer to the knowledge in relation to pro-Yahweh monotheism, and the knowledge of Yahweh as the incomparable God: thus, nobody has taught Yahweh knowledge (40.14), idol-makers do not know that the idols are no gods (44.19), Yahweh turns the knowledge of diviners into nonsense (44.25), and false knowledge of Babylon misleads her from the true God (47.10).

If all these occurrences speak about or refer to the knowledge in relation to pro-Yahweh monotheism, one can conclude that 53.11 is also a reference to the knowledge of the servant about Yahweh as the true God.[134]

---

humiliate'; M. D. Goldman ("The Root ידע and the Verb 'To Know" in Hebrew," *ABR* 3 [1953], 46-47.) as 'to put, to lay down'; H. Yalon ("לשונות ,ידע ,למד," *Tarbiz* 36 (1966-1967), 396-400) as 'to break, to smite.'

[134] This interpretation is supported by the other occurrences of the root in Is 40-53. Among the 37 occurrences, two speak about the incomparability of Yahweh with other gods (40.13, 14), two ask Israel whether they do not *know* that Yahweh is the creator (40.21,

This point is confirmed not only by the first verse of this poem ("behold, my servant *shall be wise*," 52.13), but also by the previous servant song, in which there are two occurrences of the root יָדַע: the servant has an open ear to the teaching of Yahweh (יָדַע, 50.4) and in all his humiliation he *knows* (יָדַע, 50.7) that he will not be put to shame.

The most important text that can clarify this point is 43.10 in which Yahweh presents the purpose of the election of Israel as his servant: "You are my witnesses, and *my servant* whom I have chosen, that you may *know* (יָדַע) and believe me and *understand* that *I am He* (הוא אֲנִי); before me no god was formed, nor there any after me." The redemptive knowledge of the servant, thus, is the knowledge that discerns Yahweh as the only God (see also 49.23, 26; 52.6). At the same time, idol-worshippers are said to be men devoid of knowledge (44.9, 18; 45.20; 47.11), so also the pre-exilic Israel (42.25; also 42.16).

As already mentioned more than one, the accusation against Israel raised by the Yahweh-alone party was the

---

28), four texts instruct that Israel should *know* Yahweh as the creator and the only God (41.20; 49.23; 52.6), five texts speak about the *knowledge* of Cyrus and the world about Yahweh as the only God (44.8, 45.3, 4, 5, Cyrus; 45.6; 49.26, the world), five texts speak about the *ignorance* of the idol-makers and of Babylon about the true God (44.9, 18; 45.20, 47.11[2x], 13), in three occurrences the prophet challenges gods to foretell future so that one me *know* that they are gods (41.22, 23, 26), and four occurrences accuse Israel about their *ignorance* of Yahweh's actions in history and their heard heartedness to accept him as the only God (42.25; 43.19, 48.4, 6, 7, 8[2]); therefore, he will guide them through the paths they do not *know* (42.16). In one occurrence, Yahweh judges Babylon and her gods as *ignorant* about the future things (47.8).

lack of knowledge and understanding about Yahweh, the true God: "For they are a nation void of counsel, and there is *no understanding* in them..." (Deut 32.28-29); "for Yahweh has a controversy with the inhabitants of the land. There is no faithfulness or kindness, and *no knowledge of God in the land*" (Hos 4.1); "My people are destroyed for *lack of knowledge*; for *you have rejected knowledge*, that I reject you from being a priest to me; you have forgotten the law of your God, I also will forget your children" (Hos 4.6; see also v 14; Jer 10.14; 51.17). Jeremiah foretold: "I will give you shepherds after my own heart; they will *feed you with knowledge* and understanding" (3.15). According to the Yahweh-alone party, thus knowledge about Yahweh as the only God (pro-Yahweh monotheism) is the knowledge that redeems (Is 53.11).

Now, what is the meaning of the syntagm *b^eda'tô yaṣdîq ṣadîq 'abdî lârabîm*? In fact, in Second Isaiah *ṣdq / ṣ^edāqâ* and *yš'a / y^ešû'â* (צדק and ישע) are synonyms: an examination of two texts (45.8 and 51.1-8) makes this conclusion possible. In 45.8, there is a two-fold occurrence of the root *ṣdq* and in between these two comes the root *yš'a*: "...the skies will rain down salvation (*ṣdq*); let the earth open, that salvation (*yeš'a*) may sprout forth, and *ṣ^edāqâ* ... spring up." This text uses *t^ešû'â* and *ṣ^edāqâ* as synonyms.[135]

[135] This is shown through the parallelism between the elements of the first four cola (| - | וְיִפְרוּ יֶשַׁע // הַרְעִיפוּ שָׁמַיִם | מִמַּעַל וּשְׁחָקִים | יִזְּלוּ צֶדֶק תִּפְתַּח אֶרֶץ), i.e., a b c // a' | - | c': הַרְעִיפוּ // תִּפְתַּח; שָׁמַיִם // אֶרֶץ; מִמַּעַל // - ; וּשְׁחָקִים // -; יִזְּלוּ // וְיִפְרוּ; צֶדֶק // יֶשַׁע; moreover, both, יֶשַׁע and צֶדֶק are masculine nouns which form a word-pair.

In fact, these words (צרק and ישע) appear as a pair in Isaiah 51.1-8 (3x). In v 5 these two words appear as parallels and synonyms (יָצָא יִשְׁעִי // קָרוֹב צִדְקִי): My deliverance (*ṣīdqî*) is near, my salvation (*yīš'ī*) has gone forth, and my arms will rule the peoples (שׁפט). The two following verses (vv 6, 8) consolidate this point and demonstrate that these words are interchangeable: according to v 6, even when the heaven and earth are destroyed, *y^ešû'â* of Yahweh shall remain for ever, and his *ṣ^edāqâ* shall not be abolished; whereas according to v 8 Israel should not be afraid because their enemies will be destroyed, Yahweh's *ṣ^edāqâ* shall remain for ever, and his *y^ešû'â* from generation to generation.[136]

In addition, the parallelism between 42.6 and 49.8[137] suggests that in 42.6 *ṣedeq* refers to salvation:[138] Isaiah 49.8 repeats 42.6 word by word but exchanges the two key words. According to 42.6 the servant is called in

---

[136] Verse 6, וִישׁוּעָתִי לְעוֹלָם תִּהְיֶה וְצִדְקָתִי לֹא תֵחָת;
verse 8, וְצִדְקָתִי לְעוֹלָם תִּהְיֶה וִישׁוּעָתִי לְדוֹר דּוֹרִים.

[137] אֲנִי יְהוָה קְרָאתִיךָ בְצֶדֶק וְאַחְזֵק בְּיָדֶךָ וְאֶצָּרְךָ וְאֶתֶּנְךָ לִבְרִית עָם לְאוֹר גּוֹיִם (42.6);
כֹּה אָמַר יְהוָה בְּעֵת רָצוֹן עֲנִיתִיךָ וּבְיוֹם יְשׁוּעָה עֲזַרְתִּיךָ וְאֶצָּרְךָ וְאֶתֶּנְךָ לִבְרִית עָם (49.8).

[138] Scholars usually attribute two meanings to the root, צרק: one group emphasizes the legal aspect and understands it as concurrent with a standard or norm; the second group emphasizes the redeemptive aspect of the term and understands it as a synonym of deliverance and salvation; cf. B. Johnson, " *Ṣedeq*," *TDOT* XII, 243. Dictionaries, therefore, give 'salvation' as one of the meanings of the word. For the biblical concept of *Ṣedeq and ṣ^edāqâ* cf. A. Ho, *Ṣedeq and ṣ^edāqâ in the Hebrew Bible* (AUS 78), New York, Lang, 1991; A. Niccacci, "Giustizia e giustificazione nell'Antico Testamento," *DSBP* 28, 19-106.

ṣedeq (צדק + ב = קְרָאתִיךָ בְצֶדֶק) whereas according to 49.8 in the time of salvation (יְשׁוּעָה + ב = בְּיוֹם יְשׁוּעָה) Yahweh answered his servant.

One can therefore conclude that Second Isaiah uses *ṣdq* and *yš'a* as synonyms; if they are synonyms, *ṣdq* should signify redemption as well. The two occurrences of the root *ṣdq* in 53.11 (*b^eda'tô yaṣdîq ṣadîq 'abdî lârabîm*) can therefore be interpreted / translated in the following way: *by his knowledge* (*b^eda'tô* = pro-Yahweh monotheism) *my redeemed servant* (*ṣadîq 'abdî*) *shall redeem* (*yaṣdîq*) *many*. It is through his knowledge that the servant of Yahweh is going to redeem many. For those believed in Yahweh as the only God, the exile was a vicarious suffering for the redemption of many.

The suffering servant was then the monotheistic group which grew like a small plant before Yahweh in Zion (53.2; the Yahweh-alone movement). Together with the rest of the people, they were smitten by Yahweh (cf. Hos 1.2-3; 3.1; Jer 16.1-13; 18.18; 27.1-2; 38.1-6; Lam 3 [cf. 2Chr 35.23-25] Ezek 4-5); due to the idolatry of Israel, they were also uprooted for a while (sent into exile). This group was like a lamb led to the slaughter (53.7); Jeremiah, who was one among the Yahweh-alonists, described himself as a lamb lead to the slaughter and as one who was cut off from the land of the living (11.19). In fact, in exile these people were carrying the sin of Israel and suffering (and dying - Josiah?) for them. The fellow Israelites thought that this servant was smitten by God (מֻכֵּה אֱלֹהִים וּמְעֻנֶּה). In fact, he was suffering vicariously for them, a suffering designed by Yahweh.

Through this servant figure, the prophet could also interpret the meaning of the suffering of the innocent.

Such an interpretation was also necessary because those who remained in the land seemed to have interpreted the exile as the result of the sin of this elite group which had been exiled (Ezek 11.14-21; 33.23-29).

Now who are the group of people who confess their iniquity? One can think that there were Israelites who got converted as a result of the prophetic message (cf. 51.1-8), who at last decided to go back to Zion.[139] Even though they did not understand the plan of Yahweh at first, later they recognized it and appreciated the work of the servant.

Exilic crisis could have resulted in the destruction of the Israelite religion. The suffering and knowledge of the servant, however, kept up their religious identity and made it possible to have it again; moreover, there were also Jews in Egypt, in Ethiopia, in Palestine, and elsewhere who did not go with the exiles to Babylon (Obad 20; Zeph 3.10), and thus continued to be at least monolatrous. They all now receive the new message of monotheism and exalt Yahweh as the only God. In fact, it is through the knowledge and understanding and the subsequent silent suffering of the servant-group in exile that (post-exilic) Judaism received existence and identity; thus the ancient Israelite religion grew into Judaism. Their faith could help all the Israelites to overcome the challenges against their own survival as a religious entity, without being assimilated by the surroundings.

---

[139] See a similar case in Ezra: "Rose up the heads of the fathers of Judah and Benjamin, and the priests and the Levites, *every one whose spirit God had stirred* to go up to rebuild the house of Yahweh which is in Jerusalem" (Ezra 1.5; 2.59).

III

Conclusion

The notion implied in the word "servant" necessarily points to someone (the lord) of whom he is the servant. The Isaianic notion of the servant is not an exception to this: the prophet is not presenting an isolated and abstract notion of a "servant" but he is speaking about "the servant of Yahweh." As a result, when we try to understand the Isaianic notion of the servant, it should also be connected to the Isaianic notion of Yahweh who is the lord of this servant. The servant texts in Second Isaiah should therefore be read in relation to other texts that present Yahweh as the lord. In the present work, therefore, we read the servant texts as original and integral parts of Is 40-53 and connected them with other relevant texts.

Actually there is a progressive development of the theme of the servant of Yahweh in these chapters: first the prophet presents a democratized notion of the servant of Yahweh (41.8-9); then he exposes the purpose of giving this new status to Israel which demands a rebirth of Israel (42.1-4; 43.10-13); then in the following texts it speaks about the regeneration of Israel as the servant of Yahweh; and the discussion ends with the presentation of the partial realization of the divine project in the suffering servant of Yahweh (52.13-53.12).

The servant texts should also be read as a message addressing the people in exile, which was in fact the most important period in history of the development of the Israelite religion. Bible itself gives indications to conclude that the religion of ancient Israel had undergone a process of development before it embraced an exclusive monotheistic system in exile. Knowledge about this development seems to be important in order to understand the servant passages in Second Isaiah because the servanthood of Israel is presented as a call to declare pro-Yahweh monotheism (43.10-13). In fact, Is 40-53 is the most important biblical text that discusses the motif of monotheism.

Before exile, Israel and Judah had a monolatrous notion of their God. Yahweh was the God of Israel and Judah, while the nations had their gods. According to their tradition, Yahweh had chosen Abraham and promised him to make his descendents a nation and to give them a land; later he had redeemed the offspring of Abraham from Egypt and formed them to be his chosen people; afterwards through Moses Yahweh gave them the Promised Land as a possession. In the course of history, Israel became a monarchy and Yahweh chose David as his servant and son. Yahweh promised him that his sons will reign in his throne for ever. These divine promises were important religious concepts that helped the people to live as a nation.

Notably, since the time of prophet Hosea, there seems to have emerged a monotheistic religious movement (the Yahweh-alone movement) in the North that began to think of Yahweh philosophically and to think of him as the only and true God; the advocates of this movement were theologians who emphasized the need of having the true knowledge of God; they called the people to go away from idolatry. The movement wanted to concentrate the worship of Yahweh in his Holy City, Zion. In the pre-exilic period, the movement was only a minority faction in the Israelite society.

When the Northern Kingdom was destroyed by the Assyrian emperor, the Yahweh-alone party could interpret this destruction as the result of the idolatry of the nation. This seems to have encouraged King Hezekiah to adhere to the Yahweh-alone theology. After Hezekiah, Josiah became the great advocate of the movement; in fact, he purified the nation and the cult in Jerusalem from the idols. Unfortunately, Josiah, the great champion of the Yahweh-alone party, was killed by Pharaoh Neco in 609 B.C.; subsequently, the movement lost influence in the official religion and cult. Still the movement continued to live under the leadership of people like Jeremiah and Ezekiel. For example, Jeremiah warned then that Yahweh would destroy them if they continued to be idolatrous (e.g., Jer 21.1-7).

In 586 Judah was destroyed and the upper class of the land - the religious leaders - was exiled to Babylon; then the exiled religion sought answers at least to two existential questions: 1) how to interpret the existence of the gods of the victorious nations who exalted their gods as having control of history; 2) What is the meaning of the promises of Yahweh to Abraham, Moses, and David (possession of land and eternal monarchy)? This was a critical situation and any answer given based on monolatry was unsatisfactory, because people believed that the events on earth were only the reflections of what were going on in the heavens, in the realm of the gods; this in fact brought many people to the conclusion that Yahweh had failed before the gods; moreover, the tradition had taught them that the sin of the fathers and rulers would bring disaster to their children and people from which there would be no escape.

At this critical situation Second Isaiah (an advocate of the Yahweh-alone party) got the best opportunity to announce monotheism; he interpreted the exile not as the failure of Yahweh before gods but as the result of the idolatry of Judah; he showed that the destruction was only the fulfilment of the words of the prophets of Yahweh (Is 42.23; 44.26; cf. Hos 11.5; Jer 20.4-6; 25.9-11; Ezek 12.13). For example, the Yahweh-alonist Jeremiah had advised the rulers to go away from idols and if not they would be destroyed (Jer 11.9-13); when the people were exiled to Babylon, Second Isaiah could point to the truthfulness of Jeremiah's prophecy. In fact Second Isaiah in his attempt to revitalize the religion (cf. 50.4) reinterpreted the traditional religious concepts. This seems to be the historical-religious context of the servant texts.

One of the basic problems in the religious crisis was the traditional notion of the servant of Yahweh. Abraham and Moses were the servants of Yahweh in relation to the promise of the land. In their exodus from Egypt, Moses was called the chosen servant of Yahweh (Josh 1.13; Num 12.7). He and his successor Joshua (the servant of Yahweh; Josh 5.14; 24.29) distributed the land promised by Yahweh to the Israelites. Israelites believed that the land was given to them as a perpetual possession. In the course of history, David received the title servant of Yahweh and Yahweh made a covenant with David which assured an eternal kingdom to the offspring of David.

As history moved forward, however, the great ancient Near Eastern emperors showed that their power was decisive and the people of Yahweh were dependent on them for existence and growth. Indeed, these emperors were acting as if the earthly agents of their heavenly gods. The loss of land and elimination of monarchy appeared to say that the promises of Yahweh to his servants were empty words. At this point Second Isaiah tried to reinterpret the traditional servant of Yahweh concept by democratizing it: he told the exiles that Yahweh has chosen the exilic Israel as his servant (41.8-9).

The figure of the emperor, who dominated the political and religious scene, was the best imaginable and intelligible earthly figure that could express the universal power of the only God. People already knew that it was the will of the imperial power and the faithfulness to him that decided the course of the events (cf. 2Chr 28.23). Second Isaiah, therefore, presented Yahweh (the king of Israel, 41.21; 43.15; 44.6; 52.7; 40.10) as the mighty warrior-emperor who brought kings and princes to power, who helped them or destroyed them (40.23; 41.2-4, 42.13; 49.24-25; 51.5); he visualized an international scene in which the kings and princess obeyed Yahweh's commands (43.5-7; 49.22-23), and knelt before Yahweh and sworn allegiance to him (45.23). Isaianic call to go out of Babylon (the imperial centre) is based on this new vision that Yahweh has become king and he has bared his arm before the nations (52.10-12).

After presenting Yahweh as the greatest emperor, the prophet depicted the exilic Israel as the servant / vassal of Yahweh. Notably, in the history of Israel the title servant of Yahweh was not reserved to a single person; several people received this title. Abraham and the other patriarchs who received the promise of the land were labeled as the servants (Ex 32.13; Deut 9.27-29; Ps 105.6); Moses who redeemed Israelites from Egypt and distributed the Promised Land was labeled as the servant (Josh 1.7, 13; 2King 18.12; Num 12.7); so also David who reigned this land and people, and who received the promise of an eternal kingdom was labeled as the servant (2King 20.6; Ps 89.4-5). There were also other kings (Is 22.20; Hag 2.23; 2Chr 32.16) and prophets who were given the same title (cf. 2King 9.36; 10.10; Is 20.3; 2King 14.25). In the exilic period, it was also applied to righteous persons like Job.

At the same time, according to the tradition, the labeling of one as the servant of Yahweh was always accompanied by a certain plan of Yahweh that should be actualized through this servant. In exile, when the promises of Yahweh that were given through his chosen servants appeared to be false (eternal possession of land and monarchy), Second Isaiah applied this title to all the obedient Israelites who were ready to cooperate with Yahweh's future plan of monotheism for the whole world (49.3-6). Now Yahweh has chosen Israel as his servant (41.8-9).

Reinterpreting the traditional servant concept, thus, the prophet pointed to a new future to the nation. This divine plan envisaged a future in which Yahweh through his teaching would rule all the nations from Zion, and the people of Israel would become the messengers of this great teaching (42.1-4). To have participation in this great future, the exiles have to return to Zion.

In order to prepare the people for a new exodus to their ancestral land and the city of Yahweh, the prophet outlined this servant figure like that of Moses: Moses lead the first exodus, and through him Israel came to know about Yahweh as their God; the new servant has a similar task. He will have to lead the people from the Babylonian exile and through this servant Israel will now come to the knowledge that Yahweh is the only God (monotheism).

The lord-servant metaphor was thus a prophetic rhetoric that combined both political and religious ideas; it was thus easily comprehensible to the exilic Israel. The election of Israel to be the servant of the mightiest emperor demanded total surrender and personal faithfulness on the part of the servant/vassal: he (servant) will faithfully bring forth Yahweh's rule and teaching (Is 42.3-4). It also demanded faith in a future prepared by Yahweh.

This reinterpretation implied a personalization of the religious responsibility. The election to be the servant of Yahweh demanded from the servant the right knowledge of Yahweh; this knowledge implies the conviction that he is the only God (43.10-13). The exilic Israel was actually composed of two groups: one group that recognized Yahweh as the only God (the Yahweh-alone party; 49.3; 50.4-10; 52.13-53.12), and the other group that was still blind and deaf to this knowledge (42.16, 18-19; 43.8, 10-13; 44.21-22; 49.5b; 50.11).

The prophet, who was the advocate of the first group, continuously called the second group to turn to Yahweh and be saved because there was no other God and redeemer. By employing the lord-servant metaphor, he called them to be faithful to Yahweh, because unfaithfulness on the part of the servant / vassal would lead to destruction (48.22). We can say that in the lord-servant imagery of the ancient Near Eastern political system, Second Isaiah found a lively metaphor that could express his reinterpreted notion of the servant of Yahweh in a dynamic way.

In order to realize this call to be the servant of the universal emperor, the blind Israel has to undergo a period of disciplining for which the Yahweh-alone party is the model (50.4-10). People have to undergo a formation period in which they have to come to the knowledge that Yahweh alone is God: this is a new birth of Israel for monotheism. What one sees in general in the Isaianic poems is a pendulum swinging from one point to the other: between the ideas of an already happened election, which is partially materialized in the consciously obedient life of the prophetic group (49.1-6; 50.4-10), and the objective still remaining to be achieved by all in order to realize this new status fully (42.1-4; 52.13-15; 53.10-12).

In fact, Second Isaiah really thought that Yahweh was the real lord and Israel was his servant. He therefore commanded and encouraged the people to go away from the land of Marduk and proceed to the city of Yahweh (Zion): because of the power of Yahweh (the emperor), kings and princes will fall prostrate before Israel who is the earthly executor (servant) of the divine will (41.10-15; 49.7). Nations will come to the city of Yahweh while bringing their valuable things as a gift and confessing Yahweh's power (45.14).

The exile was the result of the idolatry of the people of Yahweh. Together with the idolatrous people, in fact, the Yahweh-alone party was also exiled. This necessitated the need of explaining the exile of these 'just' people: if idolatry was the cause of exile, and Yahweh was the true God, why should these so-called righteous people suffer for that? As a good theologian, Second Isaiah also succeeded in answering this question. He presented the protagonists of this movement as the innocent who suffered for the transgression of the people (53.4). Their knowledge, however, would lead all the people to a new life/future and to the victory of the universal plan of Yahweh.

We can say that the Yahweh-alone movement which was probably initiated by Prophet Hosea -- who offered his life as a visible sign of the divinity of Yahweh against the idolatry of Israel and who declared that Yahweh desired the knowledge of God rather than burnt offerings (6.6) -- found its mature protagonist in the suffering servant of Yahweh who readily underwent discipline (50.4-5), who through his unjust exile suffered humiliation for the will of Yahweh, and who redeemed many through his knowledge (50.6-10; 52.13-53.12).

The servant of Yahweh concept in general unveils a future divine plan. This plan intends to lead the religion to a future different form the already existing one (e.g., Abraham, Moses, David, Job). The plan demands from the person called to be the servant personal responsibility and total faithfulness to God; it also demands patience and readiness to endure humiliation for the will of Yahweh. In this sense the Yahweh-alone party - Israel - is the servant of Yahweh that led the ancient Israelite religion to Judaism; in this sense Jesus is the servant of Yahweh *par excellence* because he succeeded in undergoing all humiliation for the plan of Yahweh; he opened a new future for the religion, and he succeeded in establishing a really universal and spiritual reign of the only God.

Abbreviations

Aab	Alttestamentliche Abhandlungen
ABD	*The Anchor Bible Dictionary*
ABR	*Australian Biblical Review*
ANET	*Ancient Near Eastern Texts Relating to the Old Testament*
AnBib	Analecta Biblica
AThANT	Abhandlungen zur Theologie des Alten und Neuen Testaments
AUS	American University Studies. Series VII: Theology and Religion
BA	*Biblical Archaeologist*
BAR	*Biblical Archaeology Review*
BCR	Biblioteca di cultura religiosa
BhT	Beiträge zur historischen Theologie
BiBt	Biblische Beiträge
BJRL	*Bulletin of the John Rylands University Library of Manchester*
BK	*Bibel und Kirche*
BRS	The Biblical Resource Series
BT	*The Bible Today*
BWANT	Beiträge zur Wissenschaft vom Alten und Neuen Testament. Vierte Folge
BZAW	Beihefte zur Zeitschrift für die alttestamentliche Wissenschaft
CBET	Contributions to Biblical Exegesis and Theology
CBNT	Coniectanea biblica. New Testament
CBOT	Coniectanea biblica. Old Testament Series
CBQ	*Catholic Biblical Quarterly*

CHANE	Culture and History of the Ancient Near East
COS	*The Context of Scripture*
DDD	*Dictionary of Deities and Demons in the Bible*
DSBP	*Dizionario di Spiritualità Biblico-Patristico*
DTB	Documentos en torno a la Biblia
EA	Études d'Assyriologie
EDB	Edizioni Dehoniane Bologna
EncyRel	*The Encyclopaedia of Religion*
EPROR	Études préliminaires aux religions orientales dans l'empire romain
ESNF	Edition Suhrkamp. Neue Folge
FAT	Forschungen zum Alten Testament
FB	Forschung zur Bibel
FS	Festschrift
GB	Guida alla Bibbia
HAG	Handbücher der Alten Geschichte
HKAT	Göttinger Handkommentar zum Alten Testament
HO	Handbuch der Orientalistik
HS	*Hebrew Studies*
HSS	Harvard Semitic Series
HUC	Hebrew Union College
HUCA	*Hebrew Union College Annual*
IEJ	*Israel Exploration Journal*
IMJC	The Israel Museum Jerusalem Catalogue
Interp	*Interpretation*
ITC	International Theological Commentary
JBL	*Journal of Biblical Literature*
JHNES	The Johns Hopkins Near Eastern Studies
JNES	*Journal of Near Eastern Studies*
JSJSup	Supplement to the Journal for the Study of Judaism
JSOT	*Journal for the Study of the Old Testament*
JSS	*Journal of Semitic Studies*
JTS	*Journal of Theological Studies*

LA	*Liber Annuus*
MB	Manuali di base
NKZ	*Neue Kirchliche Zeitschrift*
NZZ	*Neue Zürcher Zeitung*
OBO	Orbis Biblicus et Orientalis
OLP	*Orientalia Lovaniensia Periodica*
OTL	The Old Testament Library
OSt	Oudtestamentische Studiën
QD	Quaestiones disputatae
RB	*Revue Biblique*
RGG	*Die Religion in Geschichte und Gegenwart*
RGRW	Religions in the Graeco-Roman World
SAA	State Archives of Assyria
SBLMS	Society of Biblical Literature. Monograph Series
SBT	Studies in Biblical Theology
SELVO	*Studi Epigrafici e Linguistici sul Vicino Oriente Antico*
SRB	Supplementi alla Rivista Biblica
TBAT	Theologische Bücherei. Altes Testament
TDOT	*Theological Dictionary of the Old Testament*
TRE	*Theologische Realenzyklopaedea*
VT	*Vetus Testamentum*
WVR	Wiener Vorlesungen im Rathaus
ZAW	*Zeitschrift für die alttestamentliche Wissenschaft*

Bibliography

Ackroyd, P. R., *Exile and Restoration.* A Study of Hebrew Thought of the Sixth Century BC (OTL), London, SCM, 1968.

——, "The Temple Vessels: A Continuity Theme," in *Studies in the Religious Tradition of the Old Testament* (VTSup 23), London, Brill, 1972, 166-181.

Ahlström, G. W., "Giloh: A Judahite or Canaanite Settlement?" *IEJ* 34 (1984), 170-172.

——, *The History of Ancient Palestine From the Palaeolithic Period to Alexander's Conquest* (JSOTSup 146), Sheffield, JSOT, 1993.

Albani, M., "Deuterojesajas Monotheismus und der babylonische Religionskonflikt und Nabonid," in *Der eine Gott und die Götter.* Polytheismus und Monotheismus im antiken Israel, ed. Oeming, M. and K. Schmid (AThANT 82), Zürich, Theologischer Verlag, 2003, 171-201.

Albertz, R., "Der Ort des Monotheismus in der israelischen Religionsgeschichte," in *Ein Gott allein?* ed. Dietrich and Klopfenstein, 1994, 77-96.

——, *A History of Israelite Religion in the Old Testament Period.* vol I: From the Beginnings to the End of the Monarchy, London, SCM, 1994.

——, *A History of Israelite Religion in the Old Testament Period.* vol II: From the Exile to the Maccabees (OTL), Louisville, John Knox, 1994.

Albright, J., "Haran," *BibIl* 16 (1989), 2-3, 7-10.

Arnold, B. T., "What has Nebuchadnezzar to do with David?," in *Mesopotamia and the Bible*. On the Neo-Babylonian Period and Early Israel, ed. Chavalas, M. W. and K. L. Younger Jr. (JSOTSup 341), Sheffield, SAP, 2002, 330-355.

Avigad, N., "The Contribution of Hebrew Seals to an Understanding of Israelite Religion and Society," in *Ancient Israelite Religion*, ed. Miller, P. D., et al., 1987, 195-208.

Barré, M. L., "Textual and Rhetorical-Critical Observations on the Last Servant Song (Isaiah 52:13-53:12)," *CBQ* 62 (2000), 1-27.

Beaulieu, P.-A., *The Reign of Nabonidus King of Babylon 556-539 B.C.* (YNER 10), New Haven, Yale University, 1989.

Becking, B., "Assyrian Evidence for Iconic Polytheism in Ancient Israel?," in *The Image and the Book*, ed. van der Toorn, K. (CBET 21), Leuven, Uitgeverij Peeters, 1997, 157-172.

——, "Continuity and Discontinuity after the Exile: Some Introductory Remarks," in *The Crisis of Israelite Religion*. Transformation of Religious Tradition in Exilic and Post-Exilic Times, ed. Becking, B. and M. C. A. Korpel (OSt 42), Leiden, Brill, 1999, 1-8.

Becking, B., et al. (ed.), *Only one God?* Monotheism in ancient Israel and the Veneration of the Goddess Asherah (BS 77), Sheffield, Continuum, 2001.

Bedford, P. R., *Temple Restoration in Early Achaemenid Judah* (JSJSup 65), Leiden, Brill, 2001.

Bidmead, J., *The Akitu Festival* (GDS 2), Piscataway, Gorgias Press, 2002.

Blenkinsopp, J., *Isaiah 40-55* (AB 19A), New York, Doubleday, 2002.

Boyce, M., *A History of Zoroastrianism*. Vol I: The Early Period (HO 1, 8, 1, 2, 2A, 1), Leiden, Brill, 1975.

——, *A History of Zoroastrianism*. Vol 2: Under the Achaemenians (HO 1, 8, 1, 2, 2A, 2), Leiden, Brill, 1982.

Broshi, M., "Estimating the Population of Ancient Jerusalem," *BAR* 4 (1978), 10-15.

Browne, L. E., "A Jewish Sanctuary in Babylonia," *JTS* 17 (1916), 400-401.

Caspari, W., *Lieder und Gottessprüche der Rückwanderer* (BZAW 65), Giessen, Töpelmann, 1934.

Castel, F., *Storia d'Israele e di Giuda, dalle origini al II secolo d.C.*, seconda edizione riveduta e corretta (GB 5), Torino, Paoline, 1987.

Clauss, M., Geschichte Israels: Von der Frühzeit bis zur Zerstörung Jerusalems (587 v. Chr.), München, Beck, 1986.

Cogan, M., *Imperialism and Religion* (SBLMS 19), Missoula, Scholars Press, 1974.

Cohn, N., *Cosmos Chaos and the World to Come*. The Ancient Roots of Apocalyptic faith, New Haven, Yale University, 1993.

Conroy, C., "The 'Four Servant Poems' in Second Isaiah in the Light of Recent Redaction-Historical Studies," in *Biblical and Near Eastern Essays*, FS K. J. Cathcart, ed. McCarthy, C. and J. F. Healey (JSOTSup 375), London, T&T Clark, 2004, 80-94.

Cortese, E., *Le tradizioni storiche di Israele da Mosè a Esdra* (LB 2), Bologna, EDB, 2001.

——, "Il 'Servo di JHWH' (SdJ)," *RStB* 14 (2002), 81-98.

——, "I tentativi d'una teologia (Cristiana) dell' AT," *LA* 56 (2006), 9-28.

——, *La preghiera del Re*. Formazione, redazione e teologia dei 'Salmi di Davide' (SRB 43), Bologna, EDB, 2004.

Cowley, A., "The Meaning of מָקוֹם in Hebrew," *JTS* 17 (1916), 174-176.

Cross, F. M., *Canaanite Myth and Hebrew Epic*, Cambridge, Harvard University, 1973.

Day, J., "Asherah in the Hebrew Bible and Northwest Semitic Literature," *JBL* 105 (1986), 385-408.

——, "Yahweh and the Gods and Goddesses of Canaan," in *Ein Gott allein?* ed. Dietrich and Klopfenstein, 1994, 181-196.

de Moor, J. C., *The Rise of Yahwism* (BETL 91), Leuven, Uitgeverij Peeters, University Press, 1990.

de Vaux, R., *Ancient Israel.* Its Life and Institutions, trans by J. McHugh (BRS), Grand Rapids, Eerdmans, 1997.

de Vaux Saint-Cyr, B. C., et al., *El Siervo Doliente (Isaias 53)* (DTB 32), Estella, Verbo Divino, 2004.

Dever, W. G., "Iron Age Epigraphic Material from the Area of Khirbet el-Qôm," *HUCA* 40-41 (1969-70), 139-189.

——, "Recent Archaeological Confirmation of the Cult of Asherah in Ancient Israel," *HS* 23 (1982), 37-44.

——, "Ancient Israelite Religion: How to Reconcile the Differing Textual and Artifactual Portraits," *Ein Gott allein?* ed. Dietrich and Klopfenstein, 1994, 105-125.

Dietrich, M., "Der Werkstoff wird Gott: Zum mesopotamischen Ritual der Umwandlung eines leblosen Bildwerks in einen lebendigen Gott," *MAR* 7 (1992) 105-126.

Dietrich, M. and O. Loretz, *'Jahwe und seine Aschera'.* Anthropomorphes Kultbild in Mesopotamien, Ugarit und Israel (UBL 9), Münster, Ugarit -Verlag, 1992.

Dietrich, W. and M. A. Klopfenstein (ed.), *Ein Gott allein?* JHWH-Verehrung und biblischer Monotheismus im Kontext der israelitischen und altorientalischen Religionsgeschichte (OBO 139), Freiburg, Universitätsverlag, 1994.

Dietrich, W., "Der Eine Gott als Symbol politischen Wiederstands: Religion und Politik im Judah des 7. Jahrhunderts," in *Ein Gott allein?* ed. Dietrich and Klopfenstein, 1994, 463-490.

——, "Ueberwerden und Wesen des Biblischen Monotheismus: Religiongeschichtliche und theologische Perspektiven," in *Ein Gott allein?* ed. Dietrich and Klopfenstein, 1994, 13-30.

Dijkstra, M., "I have Blessed you by YHWH of Samaria and his Asherah: Texts with Religious Elements from the Soil Archive of Ancient Israel," in *Only one God?* ed. Becking, B., et al., 2001, 17-44.

Donner, H., *Kanaanäische und aramäische Inschriften*, vol II, Wiesbaden, Otto Harrassowitz, 1964.

——, *Geschichte des Volkes Israel und seiner Nachbarn in Grundzügen* (GATAT 4,1), Göttingen, Vandenhoeck & Ruprecht, 1984.

——, *Geschichte des Volkes Israel und seiner Nachbarn in Grundzügen* (GATAT 4,2), Göttingen, Vandenhoeck & Ruprecht, 1986.

Drijvers, H. J. W., *Cults and Beliefs at Edessa* (EPROR 82), Leiden, Brill, 1980.

Driver, G. R., "Linguistic and Textual Problems: Isaiah XL-LXVI," *JTS* 36 (1935), 396-406.

Duhm, B., *Das Buch Jesaia* (HKAT 3/1), Göttingen, Vandenhoeck & Ruprecht, 1968.

Ekblad, E. R. Jr., *Isaiah's Servant Poems According to the Septuagint.* An Exegetical and Theological Study (CBET 23), Leuven, Peeters, 1999.

Elliger, K., *Deuterojesaja in seinem Verhältnis zu Tritojesaja* (BWANT 63), Stuttgart, Kohlhammer Verlag, 1933.

Emerton, J. A., "A Consideration of Some Alleged Meanings of ידע in Hebrew," *JSS* 15 (1970), 145-188.

Emerton, J. A., "New Light on Israelite Religion: The Implications of the Inscriptions from Kuntillet `Ajrud," *ZAW* 94 (1982), 2-20.

——, "'Yahweh and His Asherah': The Goddess or Her Symbol?," *VT* 49 (1999), 315-337.

Engnell, I., "The `Ebed Yahweh Songs and the Suffering Messiah in 'Deutero-Isaiah'," *BJRL* 31 (1948), 54-93.

Fensham, F. C., "Father and Son as Terminology for Treaty and Covenant," in *Near Eastern Studies in Honor of William Foxel Albright*, ed. Goedicke, H., Batimore, Johns Hopkins University, 1971, 121-135.

Finegan, J., *Handbook of Biblical Chronology*, Princeton, University Press, 1964.

Fischer, J., *Isaias 40-55 und die Perikopen vom Gottesknecht.* Eine kritisch-exegetische Studie (AAb 6,4-5), Münster, Aschendorffsche Verlagsbuchhandlung, 1916.

——, *Wer ist der Ebed in den Perikopen Js 42,1-7; 49,1-9a; 50,4-9; 52,13-53,12?*, (AAb 8,5), Münster, Aschendorffschen Verlagsbuchhandlung, 1922.

Fowler, J. D., *Theophoric Personal Names in Ancient Hebrew* (JSOTSup 49), Sheffield, JSOT, 1988.

Freedman, D. N., "Yahweh of Samaria and His Asherah," *BA* 50 (1987), 241-249.

Fuchs, A., *Die Inschriften Sargons II aus Khorsabad*, Göttingen, Cuvillier Verlag, 1993.

Gadd, C. J., "Inscribed Prisms of Sargon II from Nimrud," *Iraq* 16 (1954), 173-201.

Galling, K., *Studien zur Geschichte Israels im persischen Zeitalter*, Tübingen, Mohr/Siebeck, 1964.

Gardiner, A., *Egypt of the Pharoahs*, London, Clarendon, 1961.

Ginsberg, H. L., "The Arm of Yhwh in Isaiah 51-63 and the Text of Is 53.10-11," *JBL* 77 (1958), 152-56.

Glueck, N., *The Other Side of the Jordan*, Cambridge, American Schools of Oriental Research, 1970.

Gnuse, R. K., *No Other Gods*. Emergent Monotheism in Israel (JSOTSup 241), Sheffield, SAP, 1997.

Goldman, M. D., "The Root ידע and the Verb 'To Know' in Hebrew," *ABR* 3 (1953), 46-47.

Goulder, M. D., "Behold My Servant Jehoiachin," *VT* 52 (2002), 175-190.

Hadley, J. M., "The Khirbet el-Qôm Inscription," *VT* (1987), 50-62.

——, "Some Drawings and Inscriptions on Two Pithoi from Kuntillet 'Ajrud," *VT* 37 (1987) 180-213.

——, "Yahweh and 'His Asherah': Archaeological and Textual Evidence for the Cult of the Goddess," in *Ein Gott allein?* ed. Dietrich and Klopfenstein, 1994, 235-268.

Handy, L. K., "Hezekiah's Unlikely Reform," *ZAW* 100 (1988), 111-115.

Haran, M., "The Disappearence of the Ark," *IEJ* 13 (1963), 46-58.

Hartmann, B., "Monotheismus in Mesopotamien?," in *Monotheismus im Alten Israel und seiner Umwelt*, ed. Keel, O., et al. (BB 14), Fribourg, Schweizerisches Katholische Bibelwerk, 1980, 49-81.

Hennessy, J. B., "Excavations at Samaria-Sebaste, 1968," *Levant* 2 (1970), 1-21.

Hentschel, G., "Elija und der Kult des Baal," in *Gott, der Einzige*. Zur Entstehung des Monotheismus in Israel, ed. Haag, E. (QD 104), Freiburg, Herder, 1985, 54-90.

Ho, A., *ṣedeq and ṣedāqâ in the Hebrew Bible* (AUS 78), New York, Lang, 1991.

Hoppe, L. J., *The Synagogues and Churches of Ancient Palestine*, Collegeville, Liturgical Press, 1994.

Huffmon, H. B., "The Covenant Lawsuit in the Prophets," *JBL* 78 (1959), 285-295.

Hugenberger, G. P., "The Servant of the Lord in the 'Servant Songs' of Isaiah: A Second Moses Figure," in *The Lord's Anointed.* Interpretation of the Old Testament Messianic Texts, ed. Satterthwaite, P. E., et al. (THS), Carlisle, Paternoster, 1995, 105-140.

Jacobsen, T., *The Treasures of Darkness*. A History of Mesopotamian Religion, New Haven, Yale University, 1976.

Jeremias, J., "Der Begriff 'Baal' im Hoseabuch und seine Wirkungsgeschichte," in *Hosea und Amos*. Studien zu den Anfängen des Dodekapropheton, ed. Jeremias, J. (FAT 13), Tübingen, Mohr/Siebeck, 1996, 86-103.

Kalluveettil, P., *Declaration and Covenant*. A Comprehensive Review of Covenant Formulae From the Old Testament and the Ancient Near East (AnBib 88), Rome, PIB, 1982.

Kittel, R., "Cyrus und Deuterojesaja," *ZAW* 18 (1898), 149-162.

——, *Jesaja 53 und der leidende Messias im Alten Testament*. Geschichte des Volkes Israel (HAG III), Gotha, Klotz, 1929.

Klein, H., "Der Beweis der Einzigkeit Jahwes bei Deuterojesaja," *VT* 35 (1985), 267-73.

Knight, G. A. F., *Servant Theology*. A Commentary on the Book of Isaiah 40-55 (ITC 29/2), Grand Rapids, Edinburgh, Eerdmans, 1984

Korpel, M. C. A., "Second Isaiah's Coping with the Religious Crisis," in *The Crisis of Israelite Religion*, ed. Becking, B. and M. C. A. Korpel (OSt 42), Leiden, Brill, 1999, 90-114.

——, "Asherah Outside Israel," in *Only one God?* ed. Becking, B., et al., 2001, 127-150.

Kramer, S. N., "Kingship in Sumer and Akkad: The Ideal King," in *Le palais et la royauté.* archéologie et civilisation, ed. Garelli, P., Paris, Paul Geuthner, 1974, 163-176.

Kraus, H.-J., *Das Evangelium der unbekannten Propheten* (KBB), Neukirchen-Vluyn, Neukirchener Verlag, 1990.

Laato, A., "The Composition of Isaiah 40-55," *JBL* 109 (1990), 207-228.

——, *The Servant of YHWH and Cyrus* (CBOT 35), Stockolm, Almqvist & Wiksell, 1992.

Labat, R., *Le caractère religieux de la royauté assyro-babylonienne*, vol 1 (EA), Paris, Libraire d'Amérique et d'Orient, 1939.

Lambert, W. G., "Nebuchadnezzar King of Justice," *Iraq* 27 (1965), 1-11.

——, "The Historical Development of the Mesopotamian Pantheon: A Study in Sophisticated Polytheism," in *Unity & Diversity*, ed. Goedicke, H. and J. J. M. Roberts (JHNES 7), Baltimore, Johns Hopkins University, 1975, 191-200.

Lang, B., *Monotheism and the Prophetic Minority* (SWBAS 1), Sheffield, Almond, 1983.

——, "Die Jahwe-allein-Bewegung," in *Der eine Gott und die Götter.* Polytheismus und Monotheismus im antiken Israel, ed. Oeming, M. and K. Schmid (AThANT 82), Zürich, Theologischer Verlag, 2003, 97-110.

Lemaire, A., "Les inscriptions de Khirbet el-Qôm et l'ashéra de Yhwh," *RB* 84 (1977), 595-608.

——, "Date et origine des inscriptions hébraiques et phéniciennes de Kuntillet `Ajrud," *SELVO* 1 (1984), 131-143.

——, "Who or What Was Yahweh's Asherah? Startling New Inscriptions from Two Different Sites Reopen the

Debate About the Meaning of Asherah," *BAR* 10 (1984), 42-51.

Levine, L. I., *The Ancient Synagogue*, New Haven, Yale University, 1999.

Lind, M. C., "Monotheism, Power and Justice: A Study in Second Isaiah," *CBQ* 46 (1984), 432-46.

Lindblom, J., *The Servant Songs in Deutero-Isaiah.* A New Attempt to Solve an Old Problem, Lund, Universitets Årsskrift, 1951.

Lipinski, E., "The Goddess Atirat in Ancient Arabia, in Babylon, and in Ugarit," *OLP* 3 (1972), 101-119.

Lipschits, O., The Fall and Rise of Jerusalem. Judah Under Babylonian Rule, Winona Lake, Eisenbrauns, 2005.

Lohfink, N., "'Israel' in Jes 49,3," in *Wort, Lied und Gottesspruch.* Beiträge zu Psalmen und Propheten, ed. Schreiner, J. and J. Ziegler (FB 2), Würzburg, Echter Verlag, 1972, 217-229.

Loretz, O., "Das Ähnen - und Goetterstatuen - Verbot' im Dekalog und die Einzigkeit Jahwehs: Zum Begriff des Goettlichen in altorientalischen und alttestamentlichen Quellen," in *Ein Gott allein?* ed. Dietrich and Klopfenstein, 1994, 491-527.

Lundbom, J. R., "The Lawbook of the Josianic Reform," *CBQ* 38 (1976), 293-302.

Malamat, A., *History of Biblical Israel* (CHANE 7), Leiden, Brill, 2001.

Mazzinghi, L., *Storia di Israele* (MB 4), Casale Monferrato, Piemme, 1992.

Mendenhall, G. E., *Ancient Israel's Faith and History.* An Introduction to the Bible in Context, Louisville, John Knox, 2001.

Meshel, Z., *Kuntillet 'Ajrud a Religious Centre From the Time of the Judean Monarchy on the Border of Sinai* (IMJC 175), Jerusalem, Israel Museum, 1978.

Meshel, Z., "Did Yahweh Have a Consort?" *BAR* 5 (1979), 24-35.

Mettinger, T. N. D., *King and Messiah*. The Civil and Sacral Legitimation of the Israelite Kings (CBOT 8), Lund, Gleerup, 1976.

——, "Die Ebed-Jahwe-Lieder: Ein fragwürdiges Axiom," *ASTI* XI (1978), 68-76.

——, "Aniconism - A West Semitic Context for the Israelite Phenomenon," in *Ein Gott allein?* ed. Dietrich and Klopfenstein, 1994, 159-178.

Na'aman, N., *Ancient Israel's History and Historiography*, Winona Lake, Eisenbrauns, 2006.

Niccacci, A., "Analysing Biblical Hebrew Poetry," *JSOT* 74 (1997), 77-93.

——, "La paternità di Dio: Linee di sviluppo dall'Antico al Nuovo Testamento," in *Mysterium regni mysterium verbi*, FS V. Fusco, ed. Franco, E. (SRB 38), Bologna, EDB, 2001, 247-271.

——, "Quarto carme del Servo del Signore (Is 52,13-53,12): Composizione, dinamiche e prospettive," *LA* 55 (2005), 9-26.

Nickelsburg, W. E., *Resurrection, Immortality, and Eternal Life in Intertestamental Judaism* (HTS 26), Cambridge, Harvard University, 1972.

Nikiprowetsky, V., "Ethical Monotheism," *Daedalus* 104 (1975), 68-69.

North, C. R., *The Suffering Servant in Deutero-Isaiah*. An Historical and Critical Study, 2nd edition, Oxford, Oxford University, 1956.

——, "The 'Former Things' and the 'New Things' in Deutero-Isaiah," in *Studies in Old Testament Prophecy*, ed. Robinson, T. H. and H. H. Rowley, Edinburgh, T & T Clark, 1950, 111-126.

——, *The Second Isaiah*, Oxford, Clarendon, 1964.

Olsson, B. and M. Zetterholm (ed.), *The Ancient Synagogue from its Origins until 200 C.E.* (CBNT 39), Stockholm, Almquist & Wiksell, 2003.

Olyan, S. M., *Asherah and the Cult of Yahweh in Israel* (SBLMS 34), Atlanta, Scholars Press, 1988.

Orlinsky, H. M., "The So-Called 'Servant of the Lord' and 'Suffering Servant' in Second Isaiah," in *Studies on the Second Part of the Book of Isaiah*, ed. Orlinsky, H.M. and N. H. Snaith (VTSup 14), Leiden, Brill, 1967, 1-133.

Parpola, S., *Assyrian Prophecies* (SAA 9), Helsinki, University Press, 1997.

Patai, R., "The Goddess Asherah," *JNES* 24 (1965), 37-52.

——, *The Hebrew Goddess*. 3rd enlarged edition, Detroit, Wayne State University, 1990.

Paton-Williams, P. W. D., "The Servant Songs in Deutero-Isaiah," *JSOT* 42 (1988), 79-102.

Patrick, D., "Epiphanic Imagery in Second Isaiah's Portrayal of a New Exodus," *HAR* 8 (1984), 125-141.

Peake, A. S., *The Problem of Suffering in the Old Testament*, London, Robert Bryant, 1904.

Polan, G. J., "Portraits of Second Isaiah's Servant," *BT* 39 (2001), 88-93.

Postgate, J. N., "Royal Exercise of Justice Under the Assyrian Empire," in *Le palais et la royauté*. Archéologie et civilisation, ed. Garelli, P., Paris, Paul Geuthner, 1974, 417-426.

Reed, W. L., *The Asherah in the Old Testament*, Fort Worth, Texas Christian University, 1949.

Robinson, T. H., *A History of Israel*, vol I: From the exodus to the fall of Jerusalem, 586 B.C., Oxford, Clarendon, 1932.

Rowley, H. H., "The Suffering Servant and the Davidic Messiah," in *Oudtestamentische Studiën*, ed. De Boer, P. A. H., Leiden, Brill, 1950, 100-136.

——, *The Servant of the Lord and Other Essays on the Old Testament*, Edinburgh, Lutterworth Press, 1952.

——, "The Servant Mission: The Servant Songs and Evangelium," *Interp* 8 (1954), 259-72.

Runesson, A., *The Origins of the Synagogue*. A Socio-historical Study (CBNT 37), Stockholm, Almquist & Wiksell, 2001.

Sanders, J. A., "The Exile and Canon Formation," in *Exile*. Old Testament, Jewish, and Christian Conceptions, ed. Scott, J. M. (JSJSup 56), Leiden, Brill, 1997, 37-62.

Schniedewind, W. M., "History and Interpretation: The Religion of Ahab and Manasseh in the Book of Kings," *CBQ* 55 (1993), 649-661.

Schroer, S., *In Israel gab es Bilder* (OBO 74), Freiburg, Universitätsverlag, 1987.

Sellin, E., *Serubbabel*. Ein Beitrag zur Geschichte der Messianischen Erwartung und der Entstehung des Judentums, Leipzig, Deichertsche Verlagsbuchhandlung, 1898.

——, *Der Knecht Gottes bei Deuterojesaja*. Studien zur Entstehungsgeschichte der jüdischen Gemeinde nach dem babylonischen Exil, Leipzig, Deichert, 1901.

——, "Tritojesaja, Deuterojesaja und das Gottesknechtsproblem," *NKZ* 41 (1930), 73-93, 145-73.

——, "Die Lösung des deuterojesjanischen Gottesknechtsrätsels," *ZAW* 55 (1937), 117-217.

Seux, M.-J., *Epithètes royales akkadiennes et sumériennes*, Paris, Letouzey et Ané, 1967.

Simons, J., *Jerusalem in the Old Testament* (SFSM 1), Leiden, Brill, 1952.

Smart, J. D., *History and Theology in Second Isaiah*, Philadelphia, Westminster, 1965.

Smith, M., *Palestinian Parties and Politics that Shaped the Old Testament*, 2nd corrected edition, London, SCM, 1987.

——, "II Isaiah and the Persians," in *Studies in the Cult of Yahweh*. Studies in Historical Method, Ancient Israel, Ancient Judaism, ed. Cohen, S. J. D. and M. Smith (RGRW 130), Leiden, Brill, 1996, 73-84, reprint from *JAOS* 83 (1963), 415-421.

Smith, M. S., "Yahweh and Other Deities in Ancient Israel: Observations on Old Problems and Recent Trents," in *Ein Gott allein?* ed. Dietrich and Klopfenstein, 1994, 197-234.

——, "Monotheism in Isaiah 40-55," in *The Origins of Biblical Monotheism*, New York, Oxford University, 2001, 179-194, 298-302.

——, *The Early History of God*. Yahweh and the Other Deities in Ancient Israel, 2nd edition (BRS), Grand Rapids, Eerdmans, 2002.

Smith-Christopher, D. L., "Reassessing the Historical and Sociological Impact of the Babylonian Exile (597/587-539 BCE)," in *Exile*. Old Testament, Jewish, and Christian Conceptions, ed. Scott, J. M. (JSJSup 56), Leiden, Brill, 1997, 7-36.

Soggin, J. A., *Storia d'Israele*. Dalle origini a Bar Kochbà (BCR 44), Brescia, Paideia, 1984.

Stolz, F., "Der Monotheismus Israels im Kontext der altorientalischen Religionsgeschichte: Tendenzen neuerer Forschung," in *Ein Gott allein?* ed. Dietrich and Klopfenstein, 1994, 33-50.

——, *Einführung in den biblischen Monotheismus*, Darmstadt, Wissenschaftliche Buchgesellschaft, 1996.

Tharekadavil, A., "Monotheism, Redemption, and the Formation of Israel as the Servant of Yahweh," Thesis ad Doctoratum, Jerusalem, SBF, 2007, 13-19

——, "How Great is This Life That You Have Given Me O Lord," *Indian Journal of Family Studies* 2 (2006), 5-15.

Theissen, G., *Biblical Faith*, trans by J. Bowden, Philadelphia, Fortress, 1985.

Thomas, W. D., "The root ידע in Hebrew," *JTS* 35 (1934), 298-306.

Tigay, J. H., *You Shall Have no Other Gods*. Israelite Religion in the Light of Hebrew Inscriptions (HSSM 31), Atlanta, Scholars Press, 1986.

——, "Israelite Religion: The Onomastic and Epigraphic Evidence," in *Ancient Israelite Religion*, ed. Miller, P. D., et al., 1987, 157-194.

Tobias, C. H., "Monotheism in Isaiah 40-55," The Faculty of New Orleans Baptist Theological Seminary, PhD dissertation, New Orleans, 1982.

Torrey, C. C., *The Second Isaiah.* A New Interpretation, New York, Charles Scribner's Sons, 1928.

Tromp, J., "The Davidic Messiah in Jewish Eschatology of the First Century B.C.E.," in *Restoration.* Old Testament, Jewish and Christian Perspective, ed. Scott, J. M. (JSJSup 72), Leiden, Brill, 2001, 191-201.

van der Ploeg, J. S., *Les chants du serviteur de Jahvé*, Paris, Gabalda, 1936.

Vorländer, H., "Der Monotheismus Israels als Antwort auf die Krise des Exils," in *Der Einzige Gott*, ed. Lang, B., et al., München, Kösel Verlag, 1981, 84-113.

Vuk, T., "Wiedererkaufte Freiheit: Der Feldzug Sanheribs gegen Juda nach dem Invasionsbericht 2 Kön 18, 13-16", Thesis ad Lauream, Pars dissertationis, SBF, 1984.

——, "Religione Nazione e Stato nel Vicino Oriente Antico e nella Bibbia," *LA* 40 (1990), 105-158.

Weinfeld, M., "Cult Centralization in Israel," *JNES* 23 (1964), 202-212.

Weippert, M., "Synkretismus und Monotheismus: Religionsinterne Konfliktbewaeltigung im alten Israel," in *Kultur und Konflikt*, ed. Assmann, J. and D. Harth (ESNF 612), Frankfurt, Suhrkamp, 1990, 143-179.

Weippert, M. H. E., "'Ich bin Jahwe' - 'Ich bin Istar von Arbela': Deuterojesaja im Lichte der neuassyrischen Prophetie," in *Prophetie und Psalmen*, FS K. Seybold, ed. Huwyler, B., et al. (AOAT 280), Münster, Ugarit-Verlag, 2001, 31-59.

Werlitz, J., "Vom Gottesknecht der Lieder zum Gottesknecht des Buches," *BK* 61 (2006), 208-211.

Whybray, R. N., *Isaiah 40-66* (NCBC), Grand Rapids, Eerdmans, 1981.

Wildberger, H., "Der Monotheismus Deuterojesajas," in *Beiträge zur Alttestamentlichen Theologie*, ed. Zimmerli, W., et al., Göttingen, Vandenhoeck & Ruprecht, 1977, 506-530, reprinted in *Jahwe und sein Volk*, ed. Schmid, H. H. and O. H. Steck (TBAT 66), München, Kaiser, 1979, 249-273.

——, "Die Neuinterpretation des Erwählungsglaubens Israels in der Krise der Exilszeit: Überlegungen zum Gebrauch von בחר," in *Jahwe und sein Volk*, FS H. Wildberger, ed. Schmid, H. H. and O. H. Steck (TBAT 66), München, Kaiser, 1979, 191-209.

Winter, U., *Frau und Göttin* (OBO 53), Freiburg, Universitätsverlag, 1983.

Winton Thomas, D., "A Consideration of Isaiah liii in the Light of Recent Textual and Philological Study," in *De Mari à Qumrân*. L'ancient testament, son mileau, ses ecrits, ses relectures juives, ed. Cazelles, H. (BETL 44), Gembloux, Duculot, 1969, 79-86.

Yamauchi, E. M., *Persia and the Bible*, Grand Rapids, Baker, 1996.

Yalon, H., "לשונות, ידע, למד," *Tarbiz* 36 (1966-1967), 396-400.

Zimmerli, W. and J. Jeremias, *The Servant of God* (SBT 20), London, SCM, 1957.

Index of Biblical Texts

Deuteronomy

Joshua

Judges

1 Samuel

1 Chronicles

2 Chronicles

Ezra

Nehemiah

Job

Lamentations

Ezekiel

Daniel

Index of Authors